OUR MISSION

Discovering God's Call to Us

Robin and John McCullough-Bade

Augsburg Fortress
Minneapolis

*This book is dedicated to our parents, who instilled in us a vision,
and to Michael, who inspires us toward a greater horizon*

OUR MISSION
Discovering God's Call to Us

Developed in cooperation with the Division for Congregational Ministries of the Evangelical Lutheran Church in America, Michael R. Rothaar, project manager.

A portion of chapter 5 is adapted from *Developing Effective Committees*, by Michael R. Rothaar, copyright © 1993, Augsburg Fortress.

Scripture quotations are from New Revised Standard Version Bible, copyright © 1989 Division of Christian Education of the National Council of the Churches of Christ in the United States of America. Used by permission.

Series overview: David P. Mayer, Michael R. Rothaar
Editors: Laurie J. Hanson, Andrea Lee Schieber, James Satter

Cover design and series logo: Marti Naughton
Text design: James Satter
Cover photograph: Gordon Gray, FRPS

About the cover image: The centerpiece of the Resurrection Window in First Lisburn Presbyterian Church, Northern Ireland, was created by stained glass artist James Watson, Belfast, from fragments of church windows destroyed by a car bomb in 1981 and restored after a second bomb in 1989. The window symbolizes new life in Christ, which transforms darkness to light, hatred to love, despair to hope, and death to life. The members of First Lisburn Presbyterian have lived out this promise through new initiatives for community service, reconciliation, and peace-making.

ISBN 0-8066-4405-2

The paper used in this publication meets the minimum requirements of American National Standard for Information Sciences—Permanence of Paper for Printed Library Materials, ANSI Z329.48-1984.

Manufactured in the U.S.A.

06   05   04   03   02   2   3   4   5   6   7   8   9   1

✚ Contents

Series Overview

Welcome to the Congregational Leader Series, and welcome to the journey of discovering God's future for you and your congregation. Your congregation's mission and ministry are given to you by God. We sometimes refer to "our church," but it is always Christ's church. We are at best its stewards or caretakers, not its owners. As we plan, organize, and lead, we strive toward excellence in everything we do to reflect the glory and grace of God, who has entered human life to redeem us.

As a congregational leader, you may be asking, "What is our mission? How should we structure things? How can we plan for the future and where will the resources come from?" The Congregational Leader Series provides resources for effective planning and leadership development. Each book includes biblical and theological foundations for planning and leadership development, and practical information to use in building on your congregation's strengths.

We are first of all called to be faithful to God's word and will. Exploring the Bible enables us to discern what God's plan is for us as individuals and as a congregation. Ignoring or minimizing the centrality of God in our deliberations risks not only failure but also our faith. In the words of the psalmist, "Unless the LORD builds the house, those who build it labor in vain"(Psalm 127:1).

Why should we engage in congregational planning and leadership development? When the congregation is at its best, these activities aid us in fulfilling our mission to the world: reaching out with the gospel of Jesus Christ. Faithful planning for mission mirrors God's activity in the world, from creating and covenant-making to gathering and renewing the church. When congregations fail to plan, they risk dissipating the resources they have been given by God and begin falling away from all that God has intended for them.

In short, faithful planning and leadership development engage the congregation and all its members in the creative work of God. Continually analyzing and shaping our vision, mission, ministry, and context allows us to ask, "What is God calling our congregation to be?" Working to develop and support leaders enables us to ask, "How has God gifted each of us for ministry?"

We begin with prayer

As congregational leaders, we always begin our endeavors with prayer. Discerning God's will for us is a task that requires that we be in communication with God. Unfortunately, we often come up with new ideas and programs—and then pray that God will bless them! That order needs to be reversed. Our prayers should precede our plans, helping us discern God's call to us.

> As congregational leaders, we always begin our endeavors with prayer.

In his few years of public ministry, Jesus accomplished a tremendous amount of healing, teaching, and service for others. However, his ministry did not begin until after he had spent an extended period of time in the wilderness reflecting on his call and God's purpose for his life. Following that retreat, virtually every moment of his life's story was punctuated with prayer and ultimately concluded with his supplications in Gethsemane and on the cross.

Paul wrote to the Thessalonians, "Rejoice always, pray without ceasing, give thanks in all circumstances; for this is the will of God in Christ Jesus for you" (1 Thessalonians 5:16-18). These words were meant for us—congregational leaders anxious to get on with things that need to be done. Notice how Paul places *prayer* between *rejoice* and *thanks* in this verse. Prayer is not simply another task to be done nor an obligation to be met. It is a gift of God to be celebrated and used with joy and thanksgiving. It is meant to permeate our lives. As leaders, we are seeking to construct God's will in our communities. God invites us to build with gladness and to make prayer the mortar between every brick we lay.

We build from strength

Most leadership resources begin with the assumption that there is a problem to be solved. In the midst of the real problems that surround us, however, our task as congregational leaders is to identify the strengths, giftedness, and blessings that God has given to us and the congregation. Our primary calling is not to be problem-solvers but to be asset-builders. Paul reminds us, "Let all things be done for building up"(1 Corinthians 14:26). This is not license to ignore problems, conflicts, or deficiencies. Rather, it is a call to view the brokenness around us in a new way.

Our primary calling is not to be problem-solvers but to be asset-builders.

Our role as Christian leaders is to attempt to look at our congregation, our fellow Christians, and ourselves, as God sees us. "This is my commandment, that you love one another as I have loved you" (John 15:12). Jesus did not blindly ignore the problems around him. Instead, he viewed those problems through a lens of love, appreciation, and forgiveness. We are called to build from strength, to construct our plans and visions from what God has given us. When we try to build from weakness and focus only on our problems, we compound both and ultimately fail.

First Church was located in a growing, well-to-do suburb, on a main thoroughfare, and in a beautiful new building. The members of First Church appeared to have everything going for them, and the congregation's future looked very bright.

The congregation, however, faced an ongoing problem with mortgage payments. This problem became so all-consuming that the congregation began to lose sight of its strengths, gifts, and mission for the future. The members of First Church had everything they needed to solve the problem of mortgage payments but they were unable to stop fixating on it. Soon, many other issues surfaced as everyone became a fault-finder.

Today there is no mortgage-payment problem because there is no First Church. The preoccupation with weakness and deficiency blinded the congregation to the reality of its gifts. This congregation died, not because of its problems but because of its perspective.

We must constantly ask ourselves and others, "Where is God at work here? What gifts have we received for ministry in this place?" Focusing only on what we don't have breeds jealousy, competition, hopelessness, and lost vision. Focusing on our gifts gives birth to joy, affirmation, and hope.

We won't find quick fixes

We live in a culture obsessed with quick fixes and mesmerized by the notion that there is a prescription for every ailment and accident. But things keep falling apart. People get sick. Programs fail. Committees don't function. Plans backfire. And goals aren't met. The list of mistakes, failures, misfires, and flops grows and grows. In his letter to the Romans, Paul reminds us that "all have sinned and fall short of the glory of God"(Romans 3:23). Paul says this not to weigh us down with despair, but instead to remind us that our salvation comes from God and not ourselves.

Faithful leaders have a deep respect for the reality of problems and obstacles. Things will always fall apart. That's why planning, assessing, goal-setting, leading, and visioning are ongoing processes, not quick fixes. As leaders, we need to know the nature of sin and publicly acknowledge its pervasiveness. Then we can lead, not with unhealthy fatalism, but with honesty, humility, and a sense of humor.

We are all ministers

As Christians, everything we do and plan is communal. We cannot plan unilaterally or devise strategies in isolation. To be sure, each of us has received salvation individually through baptism, but at that moment, through the water and the Word, we were united with the body of Christ. Even the gifts that God has given each of us are meant for the common good of all God's people: "To each is given the manifestation of the Spirit for the common good" (1 Corinthians 12:7).

In other words, each of us is a minister, whether pastor or lay person, and each of us is called to serve others. This is a radical departure from our culture's overwhelming emphasis on individual

Each of us is a minister, whether pastor or lay person, and each of us is called to serve others.

independence. The idea that we are all ministers and that as the church we minister as a community has tremendous implications for all of our planning and development efforts.

Leadership development is nothing more than equipping the members of the congregation so that they are strengthened for ministry: "The gifts he gave were that some would be apostles, some prophets, some evangelists, some pastors and teachers, to equip the saints for the work of ministry, for building up the body of Christ" (Ephesians 4:11-12). Paul would be appalled at the idea that a paid professional minister should carry out all of the ministry of the congregation or that only some people in the congregation are called to ministry.

Faithful planning and leadership development affirm that all of God's people are gifted and invited to participate in ministry. Identifying, embracing, and strengthening each other's gifts for common mission is a daunting task that never ends, but through that effort and in that journey we become what God intended: "But you are a chosen race, a royal priesthood, a holy nation, God's own people, in order that you may proclaim the mighty acts of him who called you out of darkness into his marvelous light" (1 Peter 2:9).

A model for understanding congregations

Congregations are extremely complex. Throughout the Congregational Leader Series, we invite you to look at your congregation through a particular model or set of lenses. This model helps us to understand why congregations are so complex, and it provides some important clues for the leadership skills and tasks that are needed.

A congregation resembles three different institutions at the same time: a *community of spiritual formation*, a *voluntary association*, and a *nonprofit organization*. This isn't a matter of size—the largest and smallest are alike in this. It isn't a matter of context—the model applies to both urban and rural settings. Each type of institution has different values and goals, which may even contradict each other. Each of these values and goals requires different things from leaders.

Communities of spiritual formation

A congregation is, in part, a community of spiritual formation. People come to such a community to join with others in growing closer to God. They seek to understand God's word and God's will for their life. They seek an experience of God's presence, a spiritual or emotional awareness of transcendence and love. They seek time for contemplation and prayer, and also time to work with others on tasks that extend God's love to others.

How are our congregations communities of spiritual formation? Much of congregational life centers on worship. We teach children and adults the practice of faith. The church provides support in Christ's name during times of crisis and need. We engage in visible and public activities, such as offering assistance to people who are homeless, or hungry, or survivors of abuse, as a way of both serving God and proclaiming God's mercy and justice.

> The most important value in a community of spiritual formation is authenticity.

The most important value in a community of spiritual formation is authenticity. There is no room for pretense, no room for manipulation, and no room for power games. The goals we establish must be clearly directed to outcomes in people's spiritual lives. The fundamental question for self-evaluation is this: "How has our ministry brought people closer to God?"

Voluntary associations

Like any club or voluntary association, a congregation is a gathering of people who are similar to one another in specific ways, share a common purpose, and largely govern and finance their organization's existence and activities. In addition, people often find that belonging to a club is a way to make friends and social or business contacts, and enjoy meaningful leisure time activities. Some voluntary associations, such as Kiwanis or Lions clubs, have charitable purposes and sometimes seek support from people beyond their own membership. Some voluntary associations are focused on common interests or activities, such as gardening or providing youth athletic leagues.

Membership requirements may be strict or fluid, costs may be high or low, and commitments may be long or short, but they are spelled out rather clearly. A number of unwritten rules may serve to get people to conform to common values. Most voluntary associations would like to have more members, both to strengthen their organization and to expand the social benefits that come from a broader circle. But the new members usually are people who are very much like those who are already members.

The most important value in a voluntary association is effectiveness in helping people relate to one another. The goals are largely relational. There must be many opportunities for people to form relationships, especially with those with whom they have much in common. The association must operate in such a way that people all feel that their own values and hopes are being well served, usually through direct access to the decision-making process and ample opportunities for public dissent. People want and expect to be contacted regularly by both leaders and other members, and to feel that they are fully accepted as part of the group.

> **The most important value in a voluntary association is effectiveness in helping people relate to one another.**

It is also important that there is a consensus—a shared vision—on what the association is and does. When conflict emerges, it must be negotiated and resolved. Because membership is voluntary, when there's conflict, or when they just don't feel part of the group anymore, people are usually quick to withhold their financial support or quit altogether.

Nonprofit organizations

As if it weren't complicated enough to be both a community of spiritual formation and a voluntary association, now consider that your congregation is also a nonprofit organization. It is a chartered or incorporated institution, recognized as a legal entity by the federal, state, and municipal government. A congregation can borrow and lend, sue and be sued. You as a congregation are accountable to society and responsible for following all applicable laws. Almost all congregations are property owners and employers. The congregation has formal operational procedures and documents (from your constitution to state laws) that dictate how you must make decisions and conduct your affairs. The usually unspoken but fundamental goal of a nonprofit organization is self-perpetuation, making sure that the institution will continue.

In this regard, congregations are similar to any business that offers services to the public. Being *nonprofit* simply means that the organization's assets can't be distributed to individuals or for purposes contrary to the charter. It doesn't mean that the congregation can't or shouldn't be run in a businesslike manner—or that it can't accumulate assets. The actual operation doesn't differ much from that of a profit-making business. In a nonprofit organization, the primary value is efficiency, or achieving the greatest results with the least possible expenditure of resources.

Another core value is continuity, with orderly systems that must be applied by anyone who carries out the organization's work. To reach financial goals, a nonprofit organization seeks voluntary contributions and often regularizes revenue through endowments and ancillary sources of income. Efforts are made to minimize costs without sacrificing quality. The organization also tries to build reserves to meet unanticipated circumstances and periodic needs (such as replacement of depreciating assets). Policies are in place to protect the staff and volunteers, and to ensure clear and mutually agreed upon expectations. There are clear lines of accountability and each person operates within a specified scope of decision-making.

> In a nonprofit organization, the primary value is efficiency, or achieving the greatest results with the least possible expenditure of resources.

Planning in a nonprofit organization includes making the best use of property and facilities. The property is seldom an end in itself, but the goal of leadership is always to maximize its usefulness. Other organizational goals revolve around having a truly public presence, including marketing effectively, identifying the needs and wants of a particular group of people, developing a product or service that addresses those needs, and informing the target group of its desirability and availability. Nonprofit organizations must do this as surely and skillfully as those in the profit sector.

You may have heard that "you shouldn't be a manager, you should be a leader." This is unfortunate language, because management is part of leadership, and voluntary organizations need managers. How you analyze, organize, delegate, supervise, and evaluate the congregation's work is critical to its vitality.

Leadership

What does the word *leadership* really mean? Think of it as having three dimensions: *character*, *knowledge*, and *action*. *Character* permeates all three aspects of this model. Leaders have principles and try to live them out. In any of the three ways in which we're looking at congregations, leaders are honest, trustworthy, dedicated, caring, disciplined, and faithful to the core principles—and have many more virtues as well. Although everyone sins and fails, be clear that improvement is expected from all leaders.

It is not only character that counts. Leaders must also know things and do things. *Knowledge* and *action* can be developed. They can be learned in books and classes or from working with people who have expertise. Things we know from one part of our experience can be applied to other parts of our lives.

Applying the congregational model

The three-part model of congregations is helpful in exploring the different things that leaders must be, know, and do in a community of spiritual formation, in a voluntary association, and in a nonprofit organization.

Problems develop when the values, goals, and leadership styles appropriate to one part of the congregational model are mistakenly applied to one of the others. It is not wrong to value authentic spirituality, effective interpersonal relationships, and operational efficiency. There are times when each of these should be given the highest priority. Recognize that your congregation probably has emphasized one of these areas at the expense of the others, and plan your way to a better balance. Embrace the wonderful complexity of congregational life and ask God to move among us to change us and renew us and rededicate us to God's own purposes.

The Congregational Leader Series

This is one of several books in the Congregational Leader Series. The entire series seeks to build on the positive, basing your planning on assets rather than deficiencies, and to focus on outcomes, enabling your congregation to make a specific and definable difference in people's lives. The series has two sets: congregational planning and leadership development. Books in this series can be used in any order, so you can get started with those books that are most helpful for you and your congregation. The reproducible tools can be used with your council, committees, planning teams, leadership groups, and other members of the congregation. Visit www.augsburgfortress.org/CLS to download and customize these tools.

This image of a cross indicates that further information on a topic appears in another book in the Congregational Leader Series.

Faithful planning and leadership development take us on a journey, a pilgrimage, and an exploration of God's possibilities for you and your congregation. The Congregational Leader Series provides resources for your travels, as you seek God's will and guidance for you and your congregation.

Crossroads

Here the church stands.

*Between clarity of mission
and the schism of division
Here we stand.*

*Between promises which assure
and temptations that allure
Between certainty and confusion
between dreams and illusions
Here we stand.*

*Between sweet silence of peace
and the din of war's increase
Between God's promised new creation
and our human deprivation
Here the church stands.*

And here Christ stands.

*Between sin-filled confession
and grace-full redemption
Here Christ stands.*

*Between heaven and earth
between death and new birth
Between broken promises of our past
and God's kingdom come, at last
Here Christ stands.*

*Because Christ stands,
Here we stand.*

*At once, sinner and saint,
at once, courageous and all-too-faint
Here the church stands.*

Here we stand.

Here Christ stands.

— John McCullough-Bade

Preface

The approach of this book is a simple and practical one, building on common-sense tools used by many people as they make plans in their day-to-day life. A variety of creative options are offered, enabling you to customize a planning process for your setting. You are invited to develop skills to fully engage your congregation in the process of discerning God's vision for mission and implementing a strategic plan.

One essential aspect underlies all strategic planning in the church: keeping God part of the process. This sounds obvious, yet we sometimes look to the future and make our plans relying only on our human wisdom. We would do well to turn to the words of Paul to the people of Corinth: "For God's foolishness is wiser than human wisdom, and God's weakness is stronger than human strength" (1 Corinthians 1:25).

We simply cannot fully grasp all that God has in store, but we can rejoice in God's call for the church to be partners in furthering the mission of Jesus on this earth.

This book affirms the calling of God for the church—a calling to ponder, pray, and listen for God's vision. The majority of the biblical texts are taken from the book of Acts, a book that begins with the mission mandate of Jesus: "You will be my witnesses" (Acts 1:8).

We ask for the Holy Spirit's inspiration, courage, and insight, so that we might discern God's vision for the future and how our own congregation might have the sacred privilege and awesome responsibility of participating in that vision.

Thanks be to God, who invites and includes us in the vision for the future.

Introduction

"God of grace and God of glory, On your people pour your pow'r;
Crown your ancient Church's story; Bring its bud to glorious
flow'r. Grant us wisdom, grant us courage For the facing of this
hour, For the facing of this hour."

—from "God of Grace and God of Glory,"
Lutheran Book of Worship 415
text by Harry E. Fosdick, 1878-1969

"Lord, is this the time . . . ?"
—Acts 1:6

What is the time?

"What is the *time*?" How often has any one of us been asked this
common question? Our response is usually to glance at our watch
and reply in terms of hours and minutes, the chronological time.

"What is the *time*?" We are creatures shaped by time. From the
beginning of time, God created time—day and night—and fashioned
order out of chaos. God placed humankind within this created order
and gave structure to life, even setting aside a Sabbath time for rest
and worship.

We live in chronological time. Yet there are those moments that
transcend time, when time seems to stand still. Certain events occur
that forever change the rest of time. The Gospel of Mark records Jesus'
proclamation at the beginning of his ministry in Galilee: "The time is
fulfilled, and the kingdom of God has come near; repent, and believe
in the good news" (Mark 1:15). Jesus' ministry, teaching, death, and
resurrection forever changed time, in terms of our chronological
reference system (B.C. and A.D.) and in terms of our theological
understanding of time.

Over the past 2,000 years, Christians have been called to proclaim the fulfillment of time in Jesus Christ. Although the message of this proclamation is timeless and does not change, the language and form—the way we proclaim the good news of Jesus Christ—is shaped by the times and setting.

During the first century, the purpose and identity of the church—what the church was to be and what it was to be doing—seemed clear. God's mighty Spirit came at Pentecost to the huddled followers of Jesus Christ and filled them with power to preach, teach, and heal. Acts 2 tells how a scared, motley group of believers went out on fire, risking much as they proclaimed the good news of Jesus Christ.

The followers of Jesus in the early church were referred to as *ekklesia*, a Greek word meaning "gathered." How appropriate. Jesus called, gathered, and taught these first followers as his own disciples. Then Jesus sent them to all nations as witnesses to the saving and life-giving power of God.

Those early followers turned the world upside down. The church grew in spite times of trial and persecution. The suffering endured by the early church seemed to help clarify mission and purpose. The questions of that first century became:

- Am I willing to go to jail for confessing my faith in Christ?
- Am I truly willing to be burned at the stake over this man, Jesus?

The first centuries were clear, mission-oriented times for the early church. People left their jobs and homes to spread the news of Christ. There was no need for a long-range strategic plan. Many people thought Jesus Christ would return any day. The mission was clear: Be witnesses for Jesus Christ. It was a daunting task, yet the early church seems to have approached it with a fiery zeal.

"What is the *time*?" Today, church statistics in the United States reveal a different scenario. Membership and worship attendance in mainline churches are maintaining or declining. Congregations once vibrant in the past are now closing their doors and selling their church buildings. Christian values are becoming less the norm in our society.

> Over the past 2,000 years, Christians have been called to proclaim the fulfillment of time in Jesus Christ.

In response to this changing context, congregation councils, vestries, and governing boards are increasingly aware of consumer attitudes. It is tempting to make decisions and plans primarily to accommodate and satisfy consumer demand. The question then becomes one of marketing: What will bring people in the door? But this is not enough.

Some congregations, perhaps with fewer resources or options, sink into discouragement and even despair, unsure of how to respond in these times. Members and leaders wonder, "What are we doing wrong?" and "Why don't visitors come back to our congregation?"

Others are simply confused and ask: "Why can't we be like the church in the first century, on fire with the Holy Spirit, growing and vibrant? What has happened to some congregations that were once bursting with energy and people?"

These questions have taken on new meaning since September 11, 2001. The tragic events of that day, as well as the actions and reactions in the world in response to the terrorists' attacks, have significantly impacted our time and will continue to do so. For Christians, the long-term implications of the tragedy and the responses to it are yet to be known. Many people have turned to communities of faith, seeking order in the midst of chaos, hope in the midst of sorrow, and meaning in the midst of senseless suffering.

Do we have the courage and conviction to be witnesses for Christ in the times in which we live?

Prior to September 11, 2001, the church faced the dangers of apathy and complacency. These challenges have certainly not gone away. We still are exhausted from a frantic pace of life, racing from one thing to the next, yet seeming to get nowhere that we want to go. Our busyness leaves us yearning for meaning on a deeper level in our lives. We hunger to be fed spiritually.

These pangs from spiritual malnourishment have become even sharper following the terrorist attacks on New York City and Washington, D.C. New questions are being asked, and the church is being challenged to proclaim God's message of hope, peace, and justice in a changing, uncertain time. Do we have the courage and conviction to be witnesses for Christ in the times in which we live?

L ord God, you have called your servants to ventures of which we cannot see the ending, by paths as yet untrodden, through perils unknown. Give us faith to go out with good courage, not knowing where we go, but only that your hand is leading us, and your love supporting us; through Jesus Christ our Lord. Amen

—from *Lutheran Book of Worship*, Evening Prayer, p. 153, copyright © Augsburg Fortress, Publishers

How will the church meet this challenge? How can individual congregations respond?

Have no doubt: God's Spirit is still moving, still active, still inspiring people to be witnesses for Christ. True, we may not fully know what the future holds, but we do know who holds the future. We have a profound message of hope and peace to proclaim to a fear-filled, war-torn world. The times are calling us to stop and ask significant questions, to discover anew our mission and purpose so that this message can be clearly heard.

As the hymn says, "Grant us wisdom, grant us courage, For the facing of this hour." Let us trust and pray for God's guidance as live out God's mission for us in this time.

Chapter 1

Strategic Planning

"You will be my witnesses in Jerusalem, in all Judea and Samaria, and to the ends of the earth."

—Acts 1:8

"Who, me?"— The mission mandate from Christ

Jesus gave the disciples a clear mandate for their lives and ministry: to be witnesses to the ends of the earth. The mandate gave purpose ("to be witnesses") and direction ("in Jerusalem, in all Judea and Samaria, and to the ends of the earth") for their mission and ministry.

Today we might speak of this mission mandate as a strategic plan, an overall approach to live out God's vision for the church. A strategic plan involves creating a vital mission statement based on God's word, establishing goals based on that mission statement, and developing an action plan to reach those goals. A strategic plan allows us to live into the future with clear direction.

"Yes, YOU!"

The church stands at a crossroads in history, and perhaps your congregation stands at a particular crossroad. Any number of factors could have brought you to this time and place—a change in pastoral leadership, a change in the neighborhood, or a desire for a clearer understanding of your congregation's mission and ministry. Perhaps there is some group in your congregation scratching their heads trying to figure out if the congregation is doing all that God intends for them to do. Maybe there is a small group, perhaps even the governing body of the congregation, that has raised a question about setting goals for future ministry and mission.

Sometimes this question does not come from the governing body but rather from a voice on the fringe. A young child might ask a prophetic question about the reason for the church. After a worship service, a visitor might pose a challenging question concerning the investment of the congregation's resources in God's mission work. Or, when key members of the congregation publicly depart to seek a vital ministry elsewhere, the silence after their departure may raise an entirely different set of questions.

In some circles, the bishop or another church leader simply says, "Get a mission statement and set some goals for ministry and mission." Whatever the reason, and however the question is prompted, affirm it as a gift from God, a nudging of the Holy Spirit.

You, in fact, might very well be that person who has experienced the early prompting of the Holy Spirit calling your congregation to contemplate and prayerfully discern its mission and ministry. If so, receive this challenge of strategic planning as a gift and blessing. Do not underestimate the work of God's Spirit as God calls upon leaders such as you to invite the congregation to set aside quality time for the discernment process.

Contemplation and discernment do take time. In fact, we need to take a significant amount of time to discern God's vision for the church in these times.

The contemplation and discernment process is really one of faith formation.

The contemplation and discernment process is really one of faith formation. God's Spirit empowers you and your congregation to be faith-filled in response to God's love made known in Jesus Christ. You seek ways to give God glory as you extend God's mission in your setting. Guided by God's Spirit, strategic planning ignites individuals and congregations as they see their role in bringing God's vision into reality. This process transforms a congregation into Christ-centered, mission-directed people of God.

God's gift of planning

As you consider the planning process for your congregation, keep in mind that planning need not be considered a foreign concept or treated like a dreaded disease. One of God's gifts to humanity is the remarkable ability to think. That magnificent gift includes remembering our past, assessing our current situation, and planning for the future.

Planning is a common part of life.

When you think about it, planning is a common part of life. We plan for vacations, educational opportunities, major purchases (such as a house or car), and special celebrations (such as weddings, anniversaries, birthday parties). So why is planning so often resisted in the congregation?

Strategic planning in the congregation

Not everyone's experience with the planning process in the congregation is positive. When the prospect of planning is mentioned, someone is bound to complain about how some plan is still gathering dust on a shelf. It is true that plans can get made and then shelved away; but this does not always need to be the case.

Unfortunately, strategic planning sessions sometimes have been used as opportunities to gripe about a variety of issues (including the pastor), and people are unable to focus on God's vision for the congregation. They use the time for a "dumping ground" of built-up frustration; perhaps they even attempt to bulldoze their personal agendas onto the congregation.

It is important to at least acknowledge some of these obstacles from the beginning of the planning process. Whatever the reasons, some congregations have a difficult time getting enthused about strategic planning. Nevertheless, we must not let these obstacles keep us from responding to God's calling to be a partner in mission.

Reasons to plan

There are many clear reasons for investing a congregation's time and energy in strategic planning.

Planning is a spiritual issue

Congregational planning starts by taking time to listen to God and discern God's vision. We cannot assume that the ways we have conducted ministry in the past are on target for today; we need to periodically pause and assess our bearings and ask whether we are still doing what God envisions for our congregation.

Seeking God's vision takes the focus away from our vision and our agendas. It places our planning process squarely where it needs to be—with God. Consequently, discerning God's vision can reveal our own short-sightedness and our lack of faith. Too often, we are content with the comforts of the here and now and aren't willing to be stretched and challenged by God's Spirit for the future.

Congregational planning starts by taking time to listen to God and discern God's vision.

Planning is a stewardship issue

We have been entrusted with the good news of Jesus and invited to extend the reign of God here on this earth. We are not supposed to hide this good news under a bushel or bury it in the ground. Instead, we are urged to use all of God's gifts in sharing that gift with others. These gifts include our time, talents, financial resources, and our ability to plan for the future.

Planning makes sense

Taking time to set goals for your congregation can focus energy and gifts in a unified direction. Members of the congregation can work as a team, supporting each other and building up the body of Christ for ministry and mission.

"For surely I know the plans I have for you, says the LORD, plans for your welfare and not for harm to give you a future with hope. Then when you call upon me and come and pray to me, I will hear you. When you search for me, you will find me; if you seek me with all your heart, I will let you find me, says the LORD."

—Jeremiah 29:11-14

B e enthusiastic about the opportunity to be part of God's vision for your congregation; that enthusiasm can spread. A strategic planning process is an important way for the congregation to allow God to infuse new life and spirit into the body of Christ that gathers in your congregation's setting.

Why would we not want to transfer the benefits of our experience in planning for the good of the congregation?

Tasks of strategic planning

There are four specific tasks in the process of strategic planning:

1. Listening and discerning

The planning process begins by setting aside time for prayer and Bible study in order to discern what God intends for the congregation.

2. Creating a mission statement

The mission statement is a concise statement that defines the purpose of the congregation. The mission of the church is defined by God and does not change: the church should serve as Christ's witness to the world.

3. Establishing goals based on the mission statement

The third step in the strategic planning process is the setting of goals based on the mission statement. Goals help us carry out the vision of God for our congregation. These goals are unique to the congregation. These goals should be *specific, measurable, attainable, realistic,* and *timely* (SMART for short). Additionally, they should operate within a certain length of time (no more than three to five years). These goals define how we live out the mission and make God's mission for us real in our lives. A reasonable number of goals should be set and then evaluated regularly.

4. Developing an action plan based on the goals

Once goals are established, a plan of action is needed. The action plan includes the *who, what, when, where,* and *how* of planning. This is where the mission gets carried out on a daily basis.

Beginning the strategic planning process

Too often a small group decides what is best for the entire congregation. From the beginning, make a firm commitment to involve the congregation in discerning God's vision. Do not rob the congregation of the healthy struggle of discernment. Keep in mind that the planning process is really a faith-forming endeavor for everyone involved. Glean from the wisdom of children, youth, men, and women. Dare with the elders to push the boundaries of mission. Seek ways to involve all the gifts of the congregation in this process:

Do not rob the congregation of the healthy struggle of discernment.

- Invite Sunday-school classes to reflect on God's purpose for the congregation. Begin by making a list of everything a congregation does (caring for people who are sick, providing a place for people to gather for worship, and so forth).

- Invite key people in the congregation to talk to Sunday-school classes about ways God has touched their lives through the ministry of the congregation.

- Invite Sunday-school classes to think of ways for the congregation to extend the love of Jesus Christ to others. Ask classes to draw pictures of the congregation reaching out to others. Display these on a bulletin board.

The church does not exist to serve itself but rather to carry out the mission of Jesus Christ. Consequently, every congregation needs to pause periodically, to remember the mission mandate given by Christ, and to concretely discern how it is being called by God to live out this mission mandate.

- Arrange for youth classes to survey the neighborhood. Provide training and adult supervision. What do people need? How could the congregation help its neighbors?

- Gather people in small groups to look at God's word using the Bible Study Series included on pages 82-94. Adapt the Bible studies to be age-appropriate for Sunday school and youth classes.

For more information on surveying your neighborhood, see Our Context: Exploring Our Congregation and Community.

- Hold "table talks." Invite youth and adults to gather around tables for conversation after worship. Assign each table group a particular issue or choose a different topic for all groups to discuss each week.

- Invite those confined to their homes by illnesses or disabilities to provide ideas and fervently pray for the strategic planning process.

- Make arrangements for the pastor to talk with elderly members about the congregation's mission. Use information gained from these interviews as part of a Sunday sermon.

- Involve your governing board in the overall decisions concerning the process of developing a strategic plan. This group can help to clarify tasks, responsibilities, and any time line constraints.

Know your congregation's climate

The *climate* is the attitude of the congregation, including the congregation's heart and spirit towards God and each other. How open will the congregation be to the process? How willing is the congregation to consider change? How does the congregation deal with conflict? Consider the climate of the congregation as you begin the strategic planning process.

Acknowledge the volunteer nature of the congregation

As you work to involve your congregation in the planning process, remember that the people involved will volunteer their gifts, skills, and time. You simply cannot mandate that a congregation show up for a planning session. On the other hand, do not underestimate people's deep desire to do God's will by responding to the genuine invitation to discern God's vision for the congregation and to be active partners in that vision.

Gather a team together

Consider who might have gifts, time, and interest in serving on a planning team. Seek to assemble a strategic planning team that represents a broad base of the congregation. Be sure to include new and long-time members, people of all ages, and both men and women. Look for people who work well with others and are respected by the congregation. Experience with a personal or business planning process is helpful. Above all, recruit people who love Christ and earnestly desire God's will for the congregation.

One option is to publish the above description in the congregation's newsletter and ask for nominations to the strategic planning team.

Be sure to seek a blessing or even formal approval for this team from your congregation's governing board. Install members of the team at a Sunday worship service.

Outside consultants

This book is designed to help you do strategic planning by using the people already available to you within your congregation. Sometimes, however, a non-member can see your situation more objectively and offer a fresh perspective, so do not rule out the benefits of outside consultants. In fact, an outside consultant might be extremely helpful if there has been a substantial amount of conflict within your congregation. Moreover, a pastor or other theologian who is not on the congregation's staff could provide prayer and theological reflections throughout the planning process.

Seek to assemble a strategic planning team that represents a broad base of the congregation.

See "Worship Resources" and "A Liturgy of Blessing and Commissioning" on pages 71-79.

Tips for the strategic planning team

1. Keep the process simple, steeped deeply in prayer. Make sure God is involved in every step of the process.
2. Give the team a name (such as Dream Team or Think Tank,).
3. Nurture enthusiasm for the task at hand.
4. Begin to review materials in this book. Consider your specific congregation when making preliminary plans. Note activities and approaches that might inspire and engage your congregation.
5. Read chapter 8 and select the time frame for your planning process. Will you use a season of the church year, a one-day planning session, an overnight retreat, or a year-long process? Be aware of the dates for school vacations and major events in the congregation.
6. Select images and themes that will excite and inspire your congregation. With flair and gusto, invite all members of the congregation to be involved in the planning process.
7. To become more visible and known to members of the congregation, consider providing temple talks at worship services. Briefly highlight current ministries or congregational blessings, or share short stories from your faith journeys.
8. Throughout the strategic planning process, provide opportunities for members to talk with you in informal settings, one-on-one conversations or in small groups. One way to do this is to publicize that you will be available to respond to questions or receive prayer-filled suggestions during a fellowship time or coffee hour.
7. Keep your congregation informed throughout the process. Publicize, publicize, publicize.

A formula for planning

Imagine that you are approaching a crossing in the road. The surroundings look familiar, but there is something new about the particular time and place. Signals are flashing, but their meaning is unclear. You are uncertain about what might be approaching and what might lie ahead. You are not sure when you should move forward.

To use a metaphor, the church is at a crossing. Some of the surrounding landscape looks familiar, but much of our context is changing or unknown. There are signals flashing, alerting us of possible dangers and new encounters, but we are unclear about what they mean. How and when shall we go forward? What shall we do?

When you were a child, you may have been taught a simple formula to use at a crossing: STOP, LOOK, LISTEN, and GO. By following that simple formula, you had the tools needed to assess the situation and hopefully move forward.

STOP, LOOK, LISTEN, and GO.

This book expands on that simple formula as a model for strategic planning for congregations:

This model for strategic planning is available on pages 80-81.

STOP to pray and discern if the congregation is doing what God intends.

Objective: To develop a climate for discerning what God intends for the congregation.

Key question: How do we involve members in discerning what God intends for the congregation?

Challenge: To not move too quickly toward the tasks of the planning process.

LOOK at God's word to understand the church's mission, one that has not changed over the centuries. In his final instructions to the disciples, Jesus gave a mission mandate: "You will be my witnesses . . . to the ends of the earth" (Acts 1:8).

Objective: To formulate a mission statement for the congregation.

Key question: What is God's mission for the church and the congregation?

Challenge: To involve as many people as possible in the study of God's word and review or development of the congregation's mission statement.

LISTEN to the mission mandate of Christ and the needs of others in establishing specific, measurable, attainable, realistic, and timely goals for the congregation.

Objective: To identify goals that move toward mission.

Key question: How is God calling the congregation to live out God's mission?

Challenge: To listen to the needs of the congregation and community.

GO to implement the strategic plan with confidence and hope in God's blessings. Go in the coming months and years, clearly focused on the mission mandate of Christ.

Objective: To implement the strategic plan.

Key question: How do we put the strategic plan into action?

Challenge: To communicate and implement the strategic plan in such a way that members of the congregation are included, involved, and supportive.

Each of these steps is detailed in chapters 2 through 5 of this book, followed by Bible studies and other tools for implementation. Using this book, you can select an appropriate approach to discerning God's vision for your congregation and implement a plan to turn the mission mandate of Christ into reality.

Chapter 2

STOP

Objective: To develop a climate to discern what God intends for the congregation.

Key question: How do we involve members in discerning what God intends for the congregation?

Challenge: To not move too quickly toward the tasks of the planning process.

> While staying with them [the disciples], he [Jesus] ordered them not to leave Jerusalem, but to wait there for the promise of the Father.
>
> —Acts 1:4

Jesus was about to ascend into heaven. His disciples gathered around him to hear his final words of commissioning and blessing. He clearly spoke the mission mandate—the strategic plan: "You will be my witnesses in Jerusalem, in all Judea and Samaria, and to the ends of the earth" (Acts 1:8).

The first step: STOP

Before the disciples left to carry out their mission, Jesus spoke a word that is often overlooked: Wait. How difficult a word this is for our culture. We live active lives full of motion and of doing. But as we enter the planning process, it is critical to STOP. Inviting the congregation to participate in an intentional planning process means disrupting "life as usual."

The most fundamental questions of strategic planning in the congregation are always about God. God's vision is where we begin and where we end. Discovering God's call to us is not a time to air gripes

We strive
to foster a
climate in the
congregation
for discerning
God's vision.

or to fight for "my way." Instead, we invite people to move from their personal desires, ideas, and needs to the realm of God. We strive to foster a climate in the congregation for discerning God's vision.

The planning process encourages people to see beyond the daily tasks of life to the bigger picture. It asks important questions about God working in our lives, and more specifically, in the life of the congregation.

A call for prayer

The planning process begins by seeking ways to loosen our human control over the congregation and open our hands, hearts, and spirits to God. Again and again, we ask, "What is God's vision for our congregation?"

Discerning God's vision for the congregation is not a kind of quick fix; in fact, the opposite is true. The process of discerning can involve a lengthy inner struggle. It calls for a congregation to be willing to critically examine its mission and ministry. Is God calling the congregation to change direction and begin new patterns of ministry? Is it possible that some beloved practices of ministry are not the will of God? Questions such as these are asked in the discerning process.

The Greek word in the Bible for this type of change is *metanoia*. Often translated as *repentance*, the word literally means "to change

---

God has called many people to new ventures, including . . .

Abraham and Sara	Mary Magdalene
Moses	The woman at the well
Samuel	Mary, Martha, and Lazarus
Mary, the mother of Jesus	Paul
Peter	All followers of Jesus

one's way." Never assume that the mission of your congregation is done or nothing needs to be changed. God may be leading you in new directions. Jesus died for something. That sacrifice was done out of a deep and passionate love for all people. Congregations are called to be extensions of the body of Christ, sharing that very love of Christ with others in bold ways. We pray in order to grow in our understanding of Christ's love and our mission to share that love.

Do not be surprised if strategic planning impacts individuals and your congregation in profound ways. Keep in mind that when God calls people, rarely is that call to stay in the same place and continue doing the same activities in the same way. God's vision usually involves risking and going forward in new ventures.

> **Never assume that the mission of your congregation is done or nothing needs to be changed.**

Ways to invite a congregation to pray

In this step, we STOP and call upon the congregation to actively engage in prayer, following the example of the first disciples of Jesus in Acts. After the ascension, the disciples returned to Jerusalem to await the promised Holy Spirit. In their time of waiting, the writer of Acts tells us that they were "constantly devoting themselves to prayer" (Acts 1:14).

Prayer prepares our hearts and minds to be open to God's will and call. Instead of telling God what we think our congregation should be doing, we stop and listen; we discipline ourselves to wait for clarity from God. Here are some suggestions for fostering and encouraging prayer in your strategic planning process:

1. Include prayers for your strategic planning in the Sunday morning prayers of the church.
2. Invite children, youth, and adults to pray daily for guidance.
3. Encourage members of the congregation to use a simple breath prayer. This type of prayer is a phrase repeated within the course of breathing. It can be prayed while walking, sitting, cleaning, and so forth. (For example, "God, what will you have us to do?" or "Christ, open my heart to your vision.")

4. Invite any members who regularly walk through the neighborhood to pray for the neighbors, businesses, nursing homes, and schools in your area as they walk. How does God want you to witness to the neighborhood?

5. Send out a prayer request through the congregation's prayer network or chain.

Prayer prepares our hearts and minds to be open to God's will and call.

6. Include prayers for your strategic planning in every public prayer (including all table blessings for congregational meals).

7. Invite families to include prayers for strategic planning in their devotional times.

8. Invite Sunday school classes to make prayer posters and display them throughout the church.

9. Invite area clergy and congregations to pray for your congregation. (Be available to pray for them as well.)

10. Invite members of the congregation to fast and pray as a way to acknowledge the seriousness of the task.

The task of waiting

For some people, a call to STOP for prayer will produce anxiety. We tend to move quickly through this first step and on to the more easily measured, traditional, concrete tasks of setting goals and developing action plans. Resist that temptation. Waiting on God is good for the spirit—our spirit. It is a humbling process; it is essential. We desperately need God to be our guide.

Pray for courage and wisdom to guide your congregation through the process of discerning God's will. Do not shortcut this and rely on your own wisdom.

Remember to pray throughout the process. You could in fact think of prayer as the thread that ties the planning process together from beginning to end.

Using gray paper or cardstock, make small "confession cards" with the words: "Confession—Ways our congregation has not been faithful to God's vision." These cards could be distributed at a worship service by the ushers or inserted in the bulletins.

Encourage people to prayerfully ponder before they write anything down, then collect the cards in offering plates. Present them to God and proclaim words of forgiveness such as:

Almighty God, we have fallen short of your vision for us as a congregation. Help us to be forgiving and compassionate with each other. Bring healing and hope to this congregation. Free us through your forgiving and compassionate Spirit to serve you with our whole hearts, minds, and spirits. We pray this in the name of Christ. Amen

Waiting allows time for confession

Stopping and waiting allows time to take stock and to acknowledge those ways in which we have not lived according to God's vision for us. This time is critical because the church, even at its absolute best, is still made up of human beings. We are a sinful lot; at times we miss the mark and fall short of God's intentions.

There is no doubt that we have put up barriers and blockades when it comes to God's mission work. We sometimes resist or block God's Spirit due to our own fears, limited vision of the future, or hard-heartedness concerning others. We may need to seek forgiveness from people in the congregation or community who have been hurt by what we have done or failed to do.

The confession in this first step is not done to lay blame, but to boldly acknowledge that we have not acted on all opportunities to share in God's mission and humbly admit that the congregation is not reaching its God-given potential. This confession can become part of a worship service.

Distribute brightly colored cards with the following printed on each card:

BLESSINGS—Ways that you and others have been blessed through the ministry of our congregation.

These "blessing cards" might be posted on a kiosk or bulletin board in the foyer of the church and more blessings might be added throughout the planning process. Offer the blessing cards to God as part of a worship service with a prayer:

Creator of all, thank you for blessing our lives through the witness of this congregation. Continue to guide and nurture us in faith. Show us ways to serve you faithfully. We pray this in the name of Jesus Christ. Amen

Waiting allows time to remember God's blessings

This first step, STOP, involves courage as we interrupt the usual flow of activities and begin asking critical questions of our congregation. But STOP also includes a hearty element of celebration. Even as we confess our sins, we boldly claim and receive the forgiving power of Christ. We are set us free for mission opportunities.

As we pause to ponder God's vision, we develop an attitude of gratitude for the many ways God blesses our lives. Thanks be to God for the bounty of God's love made known in Jesus Christ. See the "Worship Resources" tool on pages 71-73 for additional suggestions on including congregational confessions and blessings in a worship service.

Summary

1. **We call upon the congregation to pray.**

    Everyone, regardless of their age, is invited to pray every day. We pray for God to open our hearts and ears; we pray for the leaders of the congregation. We pray for the planning process in each worship service. We pray for God's Spirit to give us patience to endure this time of waiting. Then, we pray even more.

2. **We confess.**

We acknowledge falling short of God's vision for our congregation. We name as clearly as possible our shortcomings. We also provide means to speak and hear words of forgiveness, words to set us free for mission.

3. **We celebrate blessings.**

We identify ways in which God has blessed people in the congregation and the community through the ministry and life of our congregation.

Checklist

❏ Has the congregation been invited to pray for the planning process?

❏ Have the children, youth, and shut-ins been included in the invitation to prayer?

❏ Is there an element of anticipation brewing and bubbling as people hear the invitation to discern God's vision for the congregation and to be a partner with God in carrying out the mission mandate?

❏ Has a list of confessions (of falling short of God's vision for the congregation) been identified?

❏ Has the list of confessions been presented to God in a public way so that the freeing words of forgiveness might be proclaimed?

❏ Has a list of blessings been identified?

❏ Has the list of blessings been shared with the congregation and offered to God with prayers of thanksgiving?

Chapter 3

LOOK

Objective: To formulate a mission statement for the congregation.

Key question: What is God's mission for both the church and for the congregation?

Challenge: To involve as many people as possible in the study of God's word and review or development of the congregation's mission statement.

> This is what was spoken through the prophet Joel: "In the last days it will be, God declares, that I will pour out my Spirit upon all flesh, and your sons and daughters shall prophesy, and your young men shall see visions, and your old men shall dream dreams. Even upon my slaves, both men and women, in those days I will pour out my Spirit; and they shall prophesy."
>
> —Acts 2:16-18

As we see in Acts 2, the promised Spirit came to the disciples on Pentecost after prayer-filled STOPPING and waiting. There was excitement and confusion over what all of this meant.

Peter, inspired by the Holy Spirit, stood up and began to speak. The first words spoken (after assuring the crowd that the disciples were not drunk) were words from Scripture. "Look," Peter seems to say, "This is what the prophets were talking about. It's all beginning to make sense."

The second step in the planning process is to delve into Scripture to understand God's vision for the congregation.

When we arrive at a railroad crossing or an intersection, it is essential to look in both directions in order to discern what we should do next. Most of us look both ways as a matter of habit. However, we do not always look into God's word at times of discernment; yet it is in God's word that we see direction and purpose for our mission and ministry.

The second step: LOOK

The step LOOK invites as many people as possible into Bible study as a means to discern God's vision. This book includes a Bible study series to use in the discerning process. These Bible studies are designed for small groups but can be adapted for large groups.

When God sent Jesus into the world to call disciples and empower them with the Holy Spirit, what exactly did God intend for the early followers, and later the church, to do? In the Bible, we find that the overall mission of the church of Christ has not changed through the centuries. The mission of the church is the same at all times and in all places: to be witnesses to the saving and grace-filled love of God in Jesus Christ. How that mission mandate (or mission statement) is lived out and enacted—the goals and action plan that flow out of the mission statement—will be specific to a particular congregation and setting, but the mission mandate is universal.

See the "Bible Study Series for Small Groups," pages 82-94.

The mission of the church is the same at all times and in all places.

Claiming God's mission for a congregation

Even though the overall mission established by Jesus has not changed, specific ways to express that mission vary among congregations. A well-constructed mission statement provides a clear vision for

"I give you a new command-ment, that you love one another. Just as I have loved you, you also should love one another." —John 13:34

"You will be my witnesses in Jerusalem, in all Judea and Samaria, and to the ends of the earth." —Acts 1:8

> Find your congregation's most recent mission statement and strategic plan and examine them.
>
> - Is the mission statement vital?
> - What was the congregation's experience with the most recent strategic plan?
> - Are people aware of this plan?

The central message of any sermon and any mission statement is the good news of Jesus Christ, which is timeless.

the congregation for many years. The words and phrases selected should make sense to members of the congregation in a way that unifies and ignites them.

In many ways, a good mission statement is much like a good sermon: It will reflect the times, yet it will also stand the test of time. The central message of any sermon and any mission statement is the good news of Jesus Christ, which is timeless. Today, we can read Peter's sermon to the first-century people of Jerusalem on that first Pentecost Sunday. (See Acts 2:14-36.) This sermon has been proclaimed throughout the centuries in rural congregations and in inner-city parishes, at youth meetings and in nursing homes. In each setting, the essential truth and message of the gospel can be found and heard. And yet, Peter in other places and times used different words and images appropriate to the context in which he found himself. He translated the message, emphasizing different aspects of the gospel story, to respond to the context in which he was doing ministry.

The events of September 11, 2001, can serve as a powerful example for us. Pastors preached very different types of sermons before the terrorist attacks than they preached in the months that followed. The message had not changed; but the context—the "times"—had. The listeners had different needs and faced different challenges. The world had changed, and thus the form and emphasis of the proclamation changed as well to address the new context.

Strong mission statements are able to do the same. They are concise, coherent, and consistent with the vision of God. They withstand the test of time and pastoral changes, and they provide a thread of continuity and vision for a congregation's ministry. At the same time, mission statements should be flexible enough to reflect the context of the congregation's ministry.

A foundation for purpose and mission

The constitution of your denomination can provide a strong foundation for your congregation's mission statement. Check with your judicatory or denominational offices to find out what is available. The *Model Constitution for Congregations of the Evangelical Lutheran Church in America* (ELCA), has the following as its Statement of Purpose:"The Church is a people created by God in Christ, empowered by the Holy Spirit, called and sent to bear witness to God's creative, redeeming, and sanctifying activity in the world" (C4.01.).

Note how the phrases in this statement are succinct and direct. The theology is specifically Christian and is consistent with the denomination's understanding of God and God's work in the world. An individual congregation could take this statement and begin to shape the phrases to reflect its particular context. The final phrase, "sent to bear witness to God's creative, redeeming, and sanctifying activity in the world," could serve as a starting point for discussion:

- How are we called to "bear witness"?

- What unique gifts does the congregation have for its witness?

- What unique challenges face this congregation?

- What does "the world" look like?

- What are the needs of the community in which we are called to serve?

The ELCA's *Model Constitution* also describes six ways that its statement of purpose is carried out. Identify what your congregation is doing to carry out the mission statement of your denomination with the "Fulfilling Our Purposes" tool on pages 95-97.

The constitution of your denomination can provide a strong foundation for your congregation's mission statement.

Constitutions are discussed further in *Our Context: Exploring Our Congregation and Community* and in *Called to Lead: A Handbook for Lay Leaders.*

Writing a mission statement

As much as it is helpful to involve a large group in the pondering of the mission statement, the final wording of a mission statement is not a large-group activity. Realistically, a small group of three to five people should be given the task of creating the mission statement from the work of the congregation. The members of this group need to be attentive listeners to the work of the Holy Spirit in the congregation and able to delicately sift through contributed words and phrases.

Once the mission statement of the congregation is written, provide ample time for it to be presented to the congregation. People need opportunities to weigh the words, ponder the implications, discuss it with others, and affirm its intent.

In writing a new mission statement or reviewing an existing one, keep the following suggestions in mind:

1. Begin with prayer and the study of the Bible. Pray for God's Spirit to guide the process.

Sample mission statements

Galilean Lutheran Church, Corpus Christi, Texas

St. Paul Lutheran Church, Baton Rouge, Louisiana

The Southwestern Texas Synod of the ELCA

God's Spirit calls us:

- to hear and proclaim the Word of God
- to live and share the love of Christ

St Paul Lutheran, a COMMUNITY that . . . Invites COMMITMENT, COMMUNICATES the gospel, CARES for others, and fosters a loving CLIMATE.

A church so deeply and confidently rooted in the Gospel of God's grace that we are free to give our lives joyfully in witness and service.

P rint the completed mission statement on a giant poster or parchment paper. Have a celebration at which everyone signs the mission statement as a sign of their commitment. The statement could be framed as the congregation's Magna Carta document.

2. Use the resources available in your denomination, such as the ELCA's *Model Constitution.*

3. Challenge all ages to reflect on God's purpose for the congregation and provide many opportunities for people to submit words and phrases that capture the mission.

4. Arrange for a public sharing of these key words and phrases. Celebrate with a congregational meal and provide time for people to compare their insights.

5. Ask three to five people to finalize the statement, based on the gathered data from the congregation.

6. Keep it simple. Aim for a sixth-grade reading level.

7. Evaluate your mission statement in light of your denomination's constitution and mission statement.

8. Provide opportunities for public hearings of the proposed mission statement. Be ready to fine-tune it until it captures the essence of the mission mandate of Jesus.

9. Provide opportunities for the congregation to approve and claim the statement.

Approval and celebration

Once the mission statement is written, bring it before the governing board and the congregation for approval. This might be done in a formal meeting with the intent of including the mission statement in the congregation's constitution. Celebrate the completion of this stage in the strategic planning process.

Living out the mission statement

Once the mission statement is affirmed, the congregation will have the important task of striving to live out its mission through goals specific to the congregation's context. Again, although the mission of the church does not change, the rich opportunities for mission and ministry do vary over time. That is why discernment and planning processes are needed.

As an expression of the priorities of the congregation and an invitation into the mission of the church, the mission statement should be included on all papers leaving the church office including bulletins, newsletters, letterheads, newspaper advertisements, and so forth. It should also be included in e-mail messages, on Web sites, and in other means of communication.

Review and discussion at the annual meeting

At each annual meeting of the congregation, include a time to discuss the mission statement. A litany based on the mission statement could be developed for the annual meeting. A sample agenda and litany follow:

Agenda item

St. Paul Evangelical Lutheran Church is a community of God's people engaged in worship, learning, witness, service, and fellowship.

Our mission is to provide spiritual renewal through worship, proclamation of the Gospel, administration of the sacraments and educational opportunities so that we affirm our unity in Christ. Through this unity we are strengthened to serve and witness to each other, the community and the world, knowing that this mutual expression of faith will lead to increased understanding, growth, leadership and opportunities for extended church family relationships.

—from bylaws of the congregation's constitution

Annual meeting litany

Pastor: God has called us to be witnesses to the good news of God's saving love in Jesus Christ our Lord. We have been gathered as a community of faith as St. Paul Evangelical Lutheran Church. As God's called people in this place at this time, do you intend to continue in the covenant God made with you in Holy Baptism, to be engaged in opportunities of worship, learning, witness, service, and fellowship?

Congregation: Yes, and we ask God to help and guide us.

P: Will you avail yourselves to the joys of worship over this next year, that we might together be renewed in body and spirit through the proclamation of the Gospel and the administration of the sacraments? Will you offer yourselves, your time, and your possessions in service to God through this congregation's ministries?

C: We will, and we ask God to help and guide us.

P: Will you enter into study, prayer, and reflection upon God's word, that we might together more faithfully know and do God's will?

C: We will, and we ask God to help and guide us.

P: Will you strive to be faithful witnesses to the gospel in this congregation, in this community, and in the world, trusting that God's Spirit will lead us to increased understanding, growth, leadership, and opportunities for strengthened relationships with God and with all God's people?

C: We will, and we ask God to help and guide us.

P: Almighty God, who has given us the will to do these things, graciously give us the strength, commitment, and compassion to perform them.

P: Let us pray. Lord God, you have called us to be your people and to serve you in this time and place. You have given us a community of faith that is St. Paul Evangelical Lutheran Church. We thank you for the many gifts we receive from your bountiful hand. Bless our promises made this day, that we might fulfill them to your glory in our ministry together. Give to all of us the joy of service and constant care and guidance. Help us all to be both willing servants and thankful recipients of ministry, that your name be glorified, your people live in your peace, and your will be done; through Jesus Christ our Lord.

C: Amen

P: Go in peace. Serve the Lord.

C: Thanks be to God.

Summary

The LOOK step in the strategic planning process invites members of the congregation to study the Bible to point the way for the mission and ministries of the congregation. Through Bible study, we return to the basics for our anchor and roots, and learn about God's loving purpose for the church made known in Christ Jesus.

1. **We study God's word.**

   Everyone in the congregation is invited and urged to study the Bible to discern God's mission mandate for the church. This mission has not changed throughout the ages.

2. **We search for words to express God's mission mandate in our own words.**

   If the congregation has a mission statement, then it is time to review it. If we do not have a mission statement, then it is time to develop one. The denomination's constitution provides a starting point and guide.

3. **We affirm (or reaffirm) and celebrate our congregation's mission statement.**

   The LOOK step can culminate in a celebration. With a clear mission, the congregation is then ready to move forward.

Checklist

❑ Has the entire congregation been invited to study God's word?

❑ Have opportunities for Bible studies been offered at a variety of times and places?

❑ Has the strategic planning team discussed the mission statement in your denomination's constitution?

❑ Has a small group been designated to compile a mission statement based on input from the congregation?

❑ Are people able to remember the mission statement and repeat it readily?

❑ Is the proposed mission statement consistent with your denomination's constitution?

❑ Has the congregation had an opportunity to affirm and celebrate its mission statement?

❑ Once affirmed, has the mission statement become part of every document, including each bulletin, newsletter, and letterhead that comes out of the church office?

Chapter 4

LISTEN

Objective: To identify goals which move toward mission.

Key question: How is God calling our congregation to live out God's mission?

Challenge: To listen to the needs of the congregation and community.

> Now when they [the people in Jerusalem] heard this [Peter's sermon], they were cut to the heart and said to Peter and the other apostles, "Brothers, what should we do?"
>
> —Acts 2:37

In the first step of the STOP, LOOK, LISTEN, and GO approach to strategic planning, we STOP the usual flow of activity and invite the congregation to fervently pray for God's guidance. We offer God our confessions for not living up to God's vision for the congregation as well as celebrate the congregation's many blessings from God. In step two, we engage as many people as possible in an in-depth LOOK into the word of God and develop a clear, concise, and coherent mission statement based on the teachings and mission mandate of Jesus.

The third step: LISTEN

This next step is to LISTEN and establish goals for the congregation. This sounds easy, but you must determine to whom does the congregation listen? That is the critical issue.

Listening to Jesus

Jesus said to the disciples, "Love one another." To understand what this means, we look to Jesus and see someone who gave his life for those he loved. He washed their feet. He included the outcasts and touched the lepers and others who were called "unclean." He ate dinner with sinners. He responded to the real needs of those around him. He brought God's love to all people. Consider the following questions as you begin to LISTEN in your community:

- Who are the outcasts?

- Who are the unclean?

- With whom would Jesus share a meal?

- How can you share God's love?

The Holy Spirit pushes us beyond our own comfort zone to respond to the needs of others.

Listening to others

A "needs assessment" is a helpful tool to do exactly what it suggests: assess the needs of people. Within the congregation, a needs assessment might be done through a written survey. Outside the congregation, this can be done through door-to-door visits, surveys, and other means. Depending on the approach, a needs assessment can be done by a special task force, youth group or committee of the congregation.

Another book in the Congregational Leader Series, *Our Context: Exploring Our Congregation and Community*, deals with this topic in detail and provides helpful suggestions on assessing the needs in your community and congregation.

The challenge of this step is to investigate the needs of people beyond your own congregation. The tendency in many congregations is to listen only to the voices of members. The Holy Spirit pushes us beyond our own comfort zone to respond to the needs of others. This might be a good time to read through Jesus' parable of the good Samaritan in Luke 10:25-37. In this parable, Jesus expands our understanding of our neighbors.

At this point in the strategic planning process, it is vital to learn more about the context or setting of your congregation:

- What neighborhood or area does your congregation serve?

- What are the needs of people in this area?

Use the tool on page 98, "Mapping the Needs of Your Neighborhood," to begin to identify the needs of those outside your congregation.

- Who will be served by the congregation?

- How will the congregation proclaim God's word and share God's love in this time and place?

- How is God calling your congregation to live out its mission?

Setting goals for a congregation

Setting goals is an important part of strategic planning. Goals are clearly defined outcomes that help a congregation live out its mission statement. Generally, goals are developed for no more than three-to-five years in the future.

Develop SMART goals. Useful goals are *specific*, not general. They identify who, what, when, where, why, and how. Goals should be *measurable*, dealing with things that can be counted such as tangible objects or observable human behavior. Goals should be *attainable* within the time allotted to achieve them, using the resources available. Goals should be *realistic* so that they have a direct effect on the situations they are meant to address. Goals also should be *timely*, appropriate to the things that matter most now.

There are a number of ways to assess needs in your community. Check the latest census statistics to find out more about the people who live in your community. What issues and needs might be present in this community?

Contact the local school or school district office and obtain a copy of the district's action plan or needs assessment. Find out what information your local Chamber of Commerce and social service agencies may be able to provide.

Canvass your congregation's neighborhood through door-to-door visits designed to find out more about the people in your area.

Use postcards and newspaper announcements to let your neighbors know about these visits in advance. Provide training for those who will be making the visits and send them out in teams of two.

In a growing neighborhood or an area where many people have no church home, a congregation might set a goal of increasing membership by two new households each month. A long-term goal can be broken down into smaller objectives in order to reach the goal. With the previous example, an objective might be to call all visitors within three days after they attend a worship service for the first time.

Involving the congregation in goal-setting

Here is one procedure for setting goals in a congregation.

1. Gather data about the congregation, neighborhood, and community.
2. Bring the data to members of the congregation through creative and varied means, such as sermons, mailings, presentations, and videos on the needs that have been identified.
3. Allow time for the congregation to prayerfully consider and process the information.
4. Invite members of the congregation to pray for the needs of the community and for guidance in being Christ's witnesses in this setting.
5. Gather for an all-congregation strategic planning session.
6. Form small groups to discuss and list possible goals. (These groups could meet before the strategic planning session. If so, the session would include these goals and time to discuss additional goals.)
7. Display all the goals generated by members of the congregation. It might be helpful to post the goals on large pieces of paper around the room and group together any goals that have similar themes.
8. Spend time in prayer as people discern God's vision for the congregation.
9. Provide an opportunity for congregational members to indicate what they see as priorities, based on Christ's mission mandate.

This can be done in a number of ways. One option is to use large sheets of paper to post all the goals that have been identified, then distribute five different colored adhesive dots (available at office supply stores) to each person. Invite people to use the dots to indicate how they would prioritize the goals. To give each person an equal voice, invite everyone in the group to place one dot on each of the top five goals that they believe God is calling the congregation to address. To indicate passion toward the goals, allow each person to place up to five dots on a single goal. To show similarities and differences in priorities, designate a certain color dot for the first priority, second priority, and so on. Ask everyone to indicate their first through fifth priorities by placing the appropriate dots on the goals.

10. Later, the strategic planning team will need to compile these goals in a systematic order. Use the discussion at the all-congregation strategic planning session as a guide to establishing goals for the congregation. Similar or repetitive goals may be combined to create more succinct goals.

Goals and the committees in your congregation

Consider how the committees, task forces, ministry teams or other groups in your congregation will be involved in carrying out the congregation's goals.

Goals can be divided into committee areas. At Galilean Lutheran Church in Corpus Christi, Texas, specific goals were divided in the following way, with dates assigned to each.

Worship
- Increase the average weekly attendance at Sunday worship to 222.
- Record Sunday worship each week and distribute to shut-ins.
- Establish weekly prayer opportunities.

Congregational care
- Create and implement a system to integrate new members to the church.
- Train congregation annually on inviting others into our Christian fellowship.

Youth

- Involve all the congregation's children and youth in at least one outdoor ministry event by the time each is confirmed.

Outreach

- Designate and emphasize two activities for major outreach efforts.
- Develop welcome packets for new neighbors.
- Train children and youth to be ambassadors in sharing their faith each spring.

Support system

- Develop an Endowment Fund.
- Create a task force to consider potential staff to assist in reaching goals.
- Develop a building use policy that provides for expanded use by non-members.

Social ministry

- Involve every member in a servant opportunity beyond our congregation each year.

Another option is to set overall goals for the congregation and more specific goals, objectives, and action plans with the committees, task forces, and ministry teams in your congregation. For example, three general goals were set at Galilean Lutheran Church for a three-year period:

- To evangelize and involve our own members so that we become faithful, committed followers of Jesus Christ.
- To expand and implement a strong children and youth program (kindergarten through 12th grade) so that children/youth become faithful, committed followers of Jesus Christ.
- To implement a multifaceted evangelism program so that others become faithful, committed followers of Jesus Christ.

The following objective for the Outreach Committee supports the third goal of evangelizing others: To offer evangelism seminars three times a year to train members of the congregation on sharing their faith.

Celebrate the work of God's Spirit in and through your congregation.

Celebration

Once goals are gathered and selected, celebrate the work of God's Spirit in and through your congregation. Take delight in the work that has been completed, particularly if there has been a struggle to discern the goals for the congregation.

Summary

1. We gather information to better understand the congregation and the community.
2. We identify specific, measurable, attainable, realistic, and timely goals that move the congregation to mission.
3. We celebrate these goals and ask for God's blessing.

Checklist

❏ Do people have new understandings of their neighborhood and community?

❏ Do all segments of the congregation feel that they have been heard?

❏ Have goals been set for the congregation?

❏ Are goals based on Christ's mission mandate and faithfulness to God's word?

❏ Has a celebration event been held to lift up the mission opportunities of these goals?

Chapter 5

GO

Objective: To implement the strategic plan.

Key question: How do we put the strategic plan into action?

Challenge: To communicate and implement the strategic plan in such a way that members of the congregation are included, involved, and supportive.

> "You will be my witnesses in Jerusalem, in all Judea and Samaria, and to the ends of the earth."
>
> —Acts 1:8

What a formidable mission statement Jesus gave his disciples— to go to Jerusalem, Judea, and Samaria, and to the ends of the earth. In the book of Acts, the account of the early church's attempts to carry out this mission mandate is filled with both exciting successes and frustrating setbacks. With the Spirit's guidance, the disciples were empowered with the courage to cross over from the security of what was known to unknown and uncharted mission territory.

In strategic planning, we have seen that it is necessary to STOP, LOOK, and LISTEN before moving forward. At this point, we have assessed the current situation and are ready to move out into new ventures.

The fourth step: GO

In the step, GO, we develop a concrete plan for implementation, turning the mission and goals into reality. Detailed strategies or action plans are developed with the specific, sequential tasks needed to reach each goal and the dates for each task to be completed. Volunteers, committees, and task forces are assigned. Funding and other necessary resources are identified.

Action plans

See the
"Action Plan
Worksheet" on
pages 99-101.

An action plan answers the following questions for each strategic planning goal:

- What needs to happen?
- How will this be done?
- Why will this be done?
- Who will implement the steps?
- Which resources will be used?
- When will the steps be completed?
- Where will the steps be completed?

What needs to happen?

The first step in developing an action plan is to break each goal down into the specific steps needed to complete the goal. Some people in your congregation may not have the gift to dream and see the big vision. But when it comes to the nuts and bolts of a goal, these people may have the gift to think in sequential, systematic ways and make things happen. Ask these people to look at the congregation's goals, gather the facts, and develop specific steps to reach the goals.

How will this be done?

What method or technique will be used to accomplish each step in the action plan? In our example, the council will review the recommended strategic plan. Will this be done at a regular meeting, special session, or council retreat?

In some cases, you may choose to let the individual or group assigned to carry out the step make the decision on how things will be done. For instance, publicizing a meeting or special event could be

If one goal is to develop a strategic plan, a number of steps could be listed in an action plan:

1. Council appoints a strategic planning team.
2. Team meets, reviews materials, and makes a recommendation on the process and time line to the Council.
3. Team publicizes the strategic planning sessions and trains leaders.
4. Team implements the plan. Congregation develops goals based on its mission mandate and the needs of the community. Strategic planning team finalizes the details of the strategic plan.
5. Council reviews the final recommended strategic plan.
6. Congregation reviews and adopts the strategic plan at its annual meeting.
7. Congregation celebrates the completion of the strategic plan with a meal following the annual meeting.

done in many ways. You could simply specify the timeline and the resources available, but let the designated person or group decide on the method.

Why will this be done?

Each step in an action plan should be done for a reason: to increase participation, inform the congregation, obtain approval, receive input or feedback, and so on. You might not write down the reasons, but make sure you know why each step is necessary.

Many people are called and needed to turn God's vision into a reality.

Who will implement the steps?

Each goal, and sometimes each step, needs to have an individual or group to oversee its implementation so that someone makes it happen. Many people are called and needed to turn God's vision into a reality. Do not assume that the pastor is the one to oversee implementation. Challenge individuals to step forward to be part of the exciting opportunities developed in the strategic plan.

If your congregation has a committee structure, it may be helpful to assign primary responsibility for each goal or step to a committee. If some goals impact the ministry of several committees, primary and secondary responsibility can be assigned. For some goals, it may be logical for primary coverage to be provided by church staff members.

Which resources will be used?

An action plan is not complete without an assessment of the resources needed.

Which resources will be needed to implement the steps in the action plan? An action plan is not complete without an assessment of the resources needed, including which resources are already available and which resources will need to be obtained.

One key resource to consider is financial backing for the steps and goals. Don't underestimate God's capacity to provide in this area. God has a way of stirring hearts to be generous and providing the means to make things happen. (Read Exodus 16 to see how God provided manna to the Israelites in the wilderness.)

When will the steps be completed?

An effective action plan includes deadlines and clear expectations concerning completion dates. Write the action plan expecting to reach the goals. Use reasonable time lines so that the goals are attainable and people don't get discouraged.

Where will the steps be completed?

For some steps, when and where both need to be spelled out. Where will a special congregational meal take place? Where will food shelf donations be collected? Where will an event for your community be held?

Overseeing the strategic plan

Respect the time and effort contributed throughout the process by keeping thorough records. Take the time to record any suggestions provided along the way.

One step in an action plan is to mail out a postcard publicizing a congregational meal held to celebrate completion of a strategic plan.

The action plan could specify that you will publicize the congregational meal (*what*) with a postcard to members (*how*) to increase attendance at the meal (*why*).

The church staff member(s) or volunteer(s) in charge of writing, designing, photocopying or printing, and mailing the postcard would be listed (*who*).

Access to a photocopy machine or printer, in addition to the dollar amount needed for supplies, postage, and copying or printing would be included as resources (*which*).

You would also specify the date when the postcard needs to be at the post office for mailing (*where* and *when*).

The strategic planning team may feel some ownership of the planning document, but at some point the team will need to officially disband. Before this happens, ensure good stewardship of the strategic plan by deciding who will make sure that the plan moves forward. Will the council or a task force take on this responsibility? Will some members of the strategic planning team continue in a new capacity and oversee the implementation of the plan? Be very clear on these matters.

Evaluation

Provide encouragement and support to those who are implementing the goals by informally checking in with them periodically. Also include clear time frames for evaluation in your action plans. Minimally, this is done at the annual meeting. Quarterly or six-month evaluations are also helpful.

Also include clear time frames for evaluation in your action plans.

Some congregations appoint a standing committee to encourage the implementation process and lift up needed adjustments to the goals or action plans. In most cases, this committee reports directly to the congregation's council or governing board.

Communication

Make sure people are aware of potential changes and the reasons for them.

Communication is essential to the life of a congregation, especially in times of change. Most likely, your newly constructed strategic plan includes some element of change. Make sure people are aware of potential changes and the reasons for them.

Communication is not just the pastor's job. If the congregation has been involved in developing the strategic plan, many people should be able to articulate the vision. Effective communication at this stage includes members of the congregation communicating among themselves about the opportunities for ministry developed in the strategic plan.

Here are some ideas for communicating with your congregation about the strategic plan.

- Include an update of progress toward the congregation's goals in the annual report.

- Appoint a long-range planning task force to oversee, communicate, and support the work of the congregation in reaching the goals.

- Make progress reports a regular part of congregation council meetings.

- Keep the goals and action plans visible. Reserve one church bulletin board for displaying signs, symbols, and photos of progress towards goals.

- Keep a photo journal of the progress towards the goals.

- Establish an annual congregational celebration (in addition to the annual meeting) that provides an update on your progress. Use presentations, artistic displays, photograph montages or other means to tell the story.

Celebration

It is an exciting time for a congregation when members have invested enough time and energy in the planning process that they not only understand the congregation's mission and goals, but believe them to be what God intends for them to do. Seek out opportunities to lift up and celebrate the mighty work of God in your midst.

Lift up and celebrate the mighty work of God in your midst.

Give thanks for the people who offer their gifts to bring the plan into fruition. Provide an update on the progress in each newsletter. Thank people for their service. Celebrate God's blessings.

Celebrate God's work in and through your congregation.

- Invite the congregation to a special worship service of celebration. Thank God for guiding the strategic planning process. Pray for God's inspiration as the congregation carries out its mission, goals, and action plans. (This could be part of a regular worship service.)

- Prepare the congregation to live out the mission mandate of Christ by creating a "wave" (like those experienced at many sporting events). Of course, a wave in the congregation begins in the waters of baptism. The leader dips his or her hand into the baptismal waters of the font and proclaims words such as "Go, be my witnesses to the ends of the earth." Then the leader points to one section of the room to begin the wave. This wave spreads across the room and involves everyone. (This might be done as part of a children's sermon, but include the whole congregation.)

- Provide a celebration meal and hang mobiles around the room that depict goals and ministry projects.

Summary

1. We develop action plans based on the goals. An action plan includes the what, *how, why, who, which, when,* and *where* of turning God's vision into reality.
2. We communicate the strategic plan, goals, and action plans to the congregation in as many ways as possible.
3. We celebrate when the goals have been reached.

Checklist

❏ Has a clear action plan been developed?

❏ Has the plan been communicated to the congregation?

❏ Has an evaluation tool been set up to keep the plan moving?

❏ Have any opportunities to celebrate been incorporated into the action plan?

Chapter 6

Moving Forward

After they [the Jewish leaders in Rome] set a day to meet with him [Paul], they came to him at his lodging in great numbers. From morning until evening he explained the matter to them, testifying to the kingdom of God and trying to convince them about Jesus both from the law of Moses and from the prophets. Some were convinced by what he said, while others refused to believe. So they disagreed with each other.

—Acts 28:23-25

Mission moments

The book of Acts is filled with stories of "mission moments," times of conversion, insight, discernment, and growth of the church. The Holy Spirit continued to move in wondrous and mysterious ways. The gospel was spread to the Jewish people, to be sure, but also to an Ethiopian official (Acts 8:26-39), a Roman centurion (Acts 10), and eventually throughout the world. Clearly, the mission mandate was being fulfilled. God was doing a new thing.

This is not to say that the new vision was readily accepted by all without question or controversy. The book of Acts is also filled with stories of resistance and controversy, confusion and conflict. The conflicts and controversies in the early church became central topics in many of Paul's letters to the early churches. (For some examples, look at Paul's letters to churches in the books of Galatians, and in 1 and 2 Corinthians.)

So it should be no surprise that the process of strategic planning will, by its very nature, stir things up. This process causes people to ask new questions and look at mission and ministry through a new lens. This is part of the blessing of the process.

Healthy conflict

During the Reformation, Martin Luther and other reformers challenged the church of their time to look at its mission and ministry through the lens of the gospel. According to Luther, everything we say and do, and all that we offer in worship, study, service, and fellowship, should be done with this question in mind: "Is the gospel being proclaimed through this activity?"

The early reformers did not shy away from controversy and conflict; nor should we. They were willing to challenge and be challenged, to question and be questioned, and to wrestle with the significant issues of the faith. We can learn from their example; we can also learn from their approach. While struggling to discern God's mission and vision for the church, Luther immersed himself in Scripture for his counsel and guidance, and he turned in prayer to the God revealed in Scripture for strength, courage, and wisdom.

Prayer and study of Scripture are constants in the strategic planning process.

The importance of prayer and Bible study in the STOP, LOOK, LISTEN, GO approach described in this book cannot be over-emphasized. Prayer does not end when the STOP step is complete, nor does the study of Scripture cease when the LOOK step is done. Prayer and study of Scripture are constants in the strategic planning process.

The topic of conflict management is addressed in greater detail in the book *Our Community: Dealing with Conflict in Our Congregation* in the Congregational Leader Series. However, a few general words are helpful at this point:

- Some conflict is to be expected in the strategic planning process. Conflict can be the "burr under the saddle" that helps to get things going. It can help us to keep asking this question: "Are we doing what God intends for this congregation?"

- Conflict usually implies a deep passion and ownership of a certain stance or position. Its presence can help clarify important issues of mission and ministry.

- True, some conflict is destructive and disruptive to the planning process, but it is also true that healthy conflict—disagreements that arise out of the struggle to discern what God is calling the congregation to be and do—can be a vehicle for the Spirit's work.

Communicating about change

Conflict management and communication are often closely related. Communication is highly important in the strategic planning process and serves as the vehicle for bringing the congregation along through the changes. Good communication must flow two ways. It involves not only letting the congregation know about the steps along the way so that there are no surprises, but also including opportunities for people to be heard.

Some conflict is to be expected in the strategic planning process.

Change leads to transformation

The strategic planning process can change the very lives of those who participate in it. Transformation can occur as we open ourselves to be shaped into agents of Christ. Are we willing to be changed as we invest the time and energy to discern and carry out God's vision?

Summary

1. Strategic planning brings about change; and change causes some resistance and conflict.
2. Healthy conflict can be constructive. It can clarify, sharpen, and focus the congregation's mission.
3. Communication is critical to the strategic planning process. Provide opportunities for people to communicate with God in Bible study and in prayer, with leaders of the congregation, and with other members.
4. Be ready to be transformed in the strategic planning process.

Chapter 7

At the Crossroads

[Peter reported to the believers in Jerusalem who criticized him for allowing Gentiles to be baptized:] "And as I began to speak [to the Gentiles], the Holy Spirit fell upon them just as it had upon us at the beginning. And I remembered the word of the Lord, how he had said, 'John baptized with water, but you will be baptized with the Holy Spirit.' If then God gave them the same gift that he gave us when we believed in the Lord Jesus Christ, who was I that I could hinder God?" When they heard this, they were silenced. And they praised God, saying, 'Then God has given even to the Gentiles the repentance that leads to life.'"

—Acts 11:15-18

The early church's story in Acts is a story at the crossroads. Time after time, followers of Christ found themselves in contexts that were different and unknown. Time after time, their understanding of neighbor, church, and God was challenged and stretched. Time after time, these believers in Christ would STOP, LOOK, LISTEN, and GO.

STOP   to pray for God's guidance
to confess failures and celebrate blessings

LOOK   to Scriptures and the Lord's teaching
to understand the church's mission

LISTEN   to the needs of the community
to one another to establish goals

GO   to communicate the good news of the
gospel to Jerusalem, Judea and Samaria,
and the ends of the earth

Lord God, you have called your servants to ventures of which we cannot see the ending, by paths as yet untrodden, through perils unknown. Give us faith to go out with good courage, not knowing where we go, but only that your hand is leading us, and your love supporting us; through Jesus Christ our Lord. Amen

—from *Lutheran Book of Worship*, Evening Prayer, p. 153, copyright © Augsburg Fortress, Publishers

And so, we conclude where we began—at a crossroads. Perhaps, in a very real sense, this is where the church has and will always stand—at the intersection of past blessings and future hopes, of past understandings and future insights.

As we stand at this time and place, we are blessed with the same power bestowed upon the early church, the power of God's Holy Spirit. This Spirit given to us in baptism is "the spirit of wisdom and understanding, the spirit of counsel and might, the spirit of knowledge and the fear of the Lord, and the spirit of joy in [the Lord's] presence" (*Lutheran Book of Worship*, p. 124).

It is this Spirit which has led you and your congregation to this place; and it is that same Spirit which will lead and guide you through this time and through all that is to come.

Trust in that Spirit.

Go.

Be Christ's witnesses to the ends of the earth.

Be Christ's witnesses to the ends of the earth.

Chapter 8

Time Frames
for Strategic Planning

Your congregation can use a variety of time frames with the four-step approach to strategic planning of STOP, LOOK, LISTEN, and GO. Four options are described here: a season of the church year, a one-day planning session, a prayer retreat, and a year-long process involving resource persons.

Before you choose a time frame to use this approach in your congregation, consider the following questions:

Mission statement

- Do you need to develop a mission statement?

- Do you need to adapt your current mission statement?

Goals

- Do you hope to establish goals in this strategic planning process or simply develop a mission statement?

- Do you hope to get your congregation moving, even a bit? (Perhaps a short process could be used to establish one-year goals, with a more in-depth process provided the following year.)

- Is your congregation ready to boldly look three to five years into the future?

Action plan

- Do you expect to develop an action plan in this strategic planning process? Remember that goals without action plans for implementation won't mean much.

Overall

- How much time do you think your congregation and its leaders are willing to invest in strategic planning?

- How clear is your congregation's understanding of the mission mandate of Christ for the church?

Four time frames

These four options all have certain advantages and disadvantages. The process for each time frame is described in greater detail in the tools section of this book.

A season of the church year

In this option, strategic planning is carried out during a season of the church year. Bible studies and discussion groups culminate with an in-depth all-congregation planning session. This option connects with the worship and life of the people and works especially well with the themes of Epiphany ("Blessed to Be a Blessing," "Discovering Mission"); Lent ("A Call to Repentance," "What is God Calling Us to Be?"); and the fall season ("Mission 101," "Mission: Possible").

See "A Season of the Church Year" on pages 102-103 for details on this process.

If Sunday worship and Sunday school are used as the primary times for planning activities, special consideration needs to be made for visitors who may feel like outsiders to the strategic planning process.

A one-day planning session

See "A One-
Day Planning
Session" on
pages 104-106.

A one-day planning session based around worship builds momentum and can work well for developing a mission statement or establishing goals. Choose a time and setting that work well for your congregation.

A one-day event limits the time available to process information. Provide additional opportunities for involvement in the strategic planning process to those unable to attend the session.

A prayer retreat

See "A Prayer
Retreat" on
pages 107-109.

A prayer retreat can be used to develop a mission statement, but works best for establishing goals. A great deal can be accomplished in 24 hours and the retreat experience can help to build relationships among the participants.

Child-care options and children's activities should be considered. Set aside time for children and youth to pray for the congregation and discuss or draw what they think the congregation should be like.

Provide additional opportunities for involvement in the strategic planning process to those unable to attend this event.

A yearlong process involving resource people

See "A Year-
long Process
Involving
Resource
People" on
pages 110-112.

This option provides extended time for in-depth study and reflection and many opportunities for congregational involvement. People such as guest speakers, other pastors, and outside consultants are invited to present aspects of the mission mandate of Christ. The challenge in this option is to sustain momentum throughout the year.

Chapter 1 Tool

Worship Resources

Prayer for the planning process

Lord God, you have called us to be your people and to serve you in this time and place. You have given us this community of faith. We thank you for the many gifts we have received from your bountiful hand. Bless the work begun in this planning process, that we might be strengthened in our mission and ministry together. Give to all of us the joy of service and your constant care and guidance. Help us all to be both willing servants and thankful recipients of ministry, that your name be glorified, your people live in peace, and your will be done; through Jesus Christ our Lord. Amen

Call to worship

Leader: In the name of the Father, and of the Son, and of the Holy Spirit.

Congregation: Amen

L: As we gather for worship, we pray that God would open our hearts and minds to a vision of God's will for us.

C: We gather with faith and hope as we seek to understand the opportunities for ministry God has set before us at the present moment.

L: We gather now for worship, knowing that as we reach out to God, God creates us anew.

C: We pray for faith and courage to go forward and embrace the mission to which God calls us.

L: "For surely I know the plans I have for you, says the LORD, plans for your welfare and not for harm, to give you a future with hope" (Jeremiah 29:11).

C: We gather as God's hope-filled people, committing ourselves to knowing and doing God's will. We gather to be empowered as Christ's witnesses in the world.

L: We gather as the body of Christ in this place to dedicate and celebrate our commitment to God's vision and mission for us. We are frail and human, yet God has invited us to discern God's vision and to put that vision into action.

C: Let us rejoice and open our hearts to God's calling, trusting that God is at work in us, enabling us both to will and to work for God's good pleasure (Philippians 2:13).

Prayers of the church

L: Lord God, you have called us to ministry and mission, and you have set before us a vision of our calling as your people. Open our hearts and minds to see your will for us as a congregation. Bless the plans that are made, that we might be inspired, equipped, and more deeply committed to be witnesses to your love and care for all people. Lord, in your mercy.

C: Hear our prayer.

L: O God, you created all things and showed your love in action in the Word made flesh, Jesus Christ. Empower us with your Spirit so that in our words and actions we might communicate your love and care for all people. Forgive us when our words or actions exclude or divide. Make us ministers of your healing, reconciliation, justice, and peace. Lord in your mercy.

C: Hear our prayer.

L: Grant us quiet hearts, that we might take time to stop amid the frantic pace of life to hear your Word. Grant us open minds that we might look and listen to your will. Grant us willing hands and feet that we might go forth to be your witnesses in the world. Lord, in your mercy.

C: Hear our prayer.

L: Into your hands, O Lord, we commend all for whom we pray, trusting in your mercy; through your Son, Jesus Christ our Lord.

C: Amen

Other petitions may be offered, each ending with the words "Lord in your mercy, hear our prayer."

Chapter 1 Tool

A Liturgy of Blessing and Commissioning

We STOP to prepare

Leader: In the name of the Father, and of the (†) Son, and of the Holy Spirit.

Congregation: Amen

L: Jesus said, "You will receive power when the Holy Spirit has come upon you; and you will be my witnesses in Jerusalem, in all Judea and Samaria, and to the ends of the earth" (Acts 1:8).

C: We give thanks for the promised gift of God's Spirit in baptism. In baptism, God calls us to be witnesses to the love and grace of Jesus Christ.

All: We gather to reflect upon God's call for our mission and ministry. We pray to be faithful followers of Christ.

We STOP to confess

L: Christ calls us to be witnesses to God's love to the ends of the earth. Yet we know that we have not been faithful to that calling. Let us confess to God our failings and faithlessness. *(Pause.)* Almighty God,

C: We confess that we have fallen short of your vision for us as a congregation. We humbly acknowledge we have not always seen our mission, heard the cries of the needy, or reached out to others. Free us through your forgiving and compassionate spirit. Empower us to serve you with our whole heart, mind, and spirit, in the name of Christ. Amen

L: Hear the good news. Through Christ's death on the cross, we are forgiven and empowered to be God's witnesses, bringing God's healing and wholeness to the ends of the earth. Arise. Look anew. Walk in the light of the Lord!

C: Thanks be to God!

Opening hymn

We STOP to give thanks to God

The following litany is based on the hymn "For the Fruit of All Creation," *Lutheran Book of Worship* 563. Text by Fred Pratt Green, 1903-2000. Words copyright © 1970 by Hope Publishing Co., Carol Stream, IL 60188. All rights reserved.

L: The grace of our Lord Jesus Christ, the love of God, and the communion of the Holy Spirit be with you all.

C: And also with you.

L: For the fruit of all creation,

C: Thanks be to God.

L: For God's gifts to every nation,

C: Thanks be to God.

L: For the plowing, sowing, reaping,

C: Silent growth while we are sleeping,

L: Future needs in earth's safekeeping,

C: Thanks be to God.

L: For the harvests of the Spirit,

C: Thanks be to God.

L: For the good we all inherit,

C: Thanks be to God.

L: For the wonders that astound us,

C: For the truths that still confound us,

L: Most of all, that love has found us,

C: THANKS BE TO GOD!

The prayer of the day

Gracious God, open our hearts and minds to your will for us. Open our eyes to see the opportunities for ministry you set before us at this present moment. Grant us faith and courage to go forward and embrace the mission to which you call us. Lead us and guide us. Grant us wisdom and discernment, and quiet and willing hearts that we might hear and know your will, through Jesus Christ our Lord. Amen

We LOOK in God's word for our mission

First Lesson: Jeremiah 29:10-14

Second Lesson: Acts 1:1-8

Gospel: John 13:1-17

Sermon

Hymn

The Apostles' Creed

The offering

The offertory

The following is sung to the tune of "Now All the Vault of Heaven Resounds," *Lutheran Book of Worship* 143

Praise God from whom all blessings flow.
Praise God, all creatures here below.
Alleluia! Alleluia!
Praise God, the source of all our gifts.
Praise Jesus Christ, whose power uplifts.
Praise the Spirit, Holy Spirit.
Alleluia! Alleluia! Alleluia!

The offertory prayer

Installation of the strategic planning team members

L: We as a congregation are embarking on an exciting journey to discern God's vision for our mission and ministry. Let us pray God's blessings on our endeavors and on those who will lead us. Let us commit ourselves to prayer, the study of Scripture, and participation in the opportunities before us.

A: The following people have been appointed to serve as members of the strategic planning team.

L: (Read Acts 2:1-4, 16-18.) You have been called to be open to God's Spirit, to help us in prayer and study of Scripture, and to assist us in discerning God's vision for our congregation and dreaming new dreams. Will you assume this ministry in the confidence that it comes from God?

Response: I will, and I ask God to help me.

L: Will you be diligent in your study of the Bible and faithful in prayer?

Response: I will, and I ask God to help me.

C: Will you work together with other members to see that the mission and ministry to which Christ calls us is done in this congregation, in the community, and in the whole world?

Response: I will, and I ask God to help me.

(Those being installed face the congregation)

L: People of God, will you support these brothers and sisters in Christ by praying for them and sharing in the mutual ministry that God has given to all the baptized?

C: We will, and we ask God to help us.

L: Almighty God, who has given you the will to do these things, now graciously give you the strength, wisdom, and compassion to perform them.

C: Amen

L: I now commission you as the strategic planning team for this congregation. God bless you with the Holy Spirit, that you may be faithful servants of Christ.

C: Amen

A = president of the congregation or an assisting minister.

Strategic planning team members come forward as their names are read.

We LISTEN to needs—We LISTEN for God

The prayers of the church

L: Let us pray for the whole people of God in Christ Jesus, and for all people according to their needs. Lord God, you have called us to ministry and mission. Open our hearts and minds to see your will for us as a congregation. Bless the plans that are made and the journey upon which we embark, that we might be inspired, equipped, and more deeply committed to be your witnesses to your love and care for all people. Lord, in your mercy,

C: Hear our prayer.

L: Be with those who serve on the strategic planning team, and grant them the gift of your Holy Spirit given to them in their baptisms: the spirit of wisdom and understanding, the spirit of counsel and might, the spirit of knowledge and fear of the Lord. Use this congregation to support the strategic planning team in its work. Lord, in your mercy,

C: Hear our prayer.

L: Grant us quiet hearts, that we might take time to stop amid the frantic pace of life to hear your word. Grant us open minds that we might look and listen to your will. Grant us caring hearts that we might hear the cries of those in need in our congregation and community. Grant us willing hands and feet that we might go forth to be your witnesses in the world. Lord, in your mercy,

C: Hear our prayer.

L: (Other petitions may be offered.) Into your hands, O Lord, we commend all for whom we pray, trusting in your mercy; through your Son, Jesus Christ our Lord.

C: Amen

The Lord's Prayer

We GO to serve the Lord

Prayer of sending

L: Let us pray.

C: Lord God, you have called your servants to ventures of which we cannot see the ending, by paths as yet untrodden, through perils unknown. Give us faith to go out with good courage, not knowing where we go, but only that your hand is leading us and your love supporting us; through Jesus Christ our Lord. Amen

—from *Lutheran Book of Worship*, Evening Prayer, p. p. 153, copyright © Augsburg Fortress, Publishers

Hymn of sending

L: Go in peace. Serve the Lord.

C: THANKS BE TO GOD!

Chapter 1 Tool

An Overview of the Strategic Planning Process

STOP to pray and discern if the congregation is doing what God intends.

Objective: To develop a climate for discerning what God intends for the congregation.

Key question: How do we involve members in discerning what God intends for the congregation?

Challenge: To not move too quickly toward the tasks of the planning process.

LOOK at God's word to understand the church's mission, a mission that has not changed over the centuries. In his final instructions to his disciples, Jesus gave a mission mandate: "You will be my witnesses . . . to the ends of the earth" (Acts 1:8).

Objective: To formulate a mission statement for the congregation.

Key question: What is God's mission for the church and the congregation?

Challenge: To involve as many people as possible in the study of God's word and review or development of the congregation's mission statement.

LISTEN to the mission mandate of Christ and the needs of others in establishing specific, measurable, attainable, realistic, and timely goals for the congregation.

Objective: To identify goals that move toward mission.

Key question: How is God calling the congregation to live out its mission?

Challenge: To listen to the needs of the congregation and the community.

GO to implement the strategic plan with confidence and hope in God's blessings. Go in the coming months and years, clearly focused on the mission mandate of Christ.

Objective: To implement the strategic plan.

Key question: How do we put the strategic plan into action?

Challenge: To communicate and implement the strategic plan in such a way that members of the congregation are included, involved, and supportive.

Chapter 3 Tool

Bible Study Series for Small Groups

Overview

The series of three Bible studies in this book is designed to gather the congregation in small groups for Bible study, prayer, and discernment concerning God's vision for the congregation. Ideally, these discussions will take place in small groups of five to ten people in the comfort of individual homes, but they can be adapted for a large group and other settings. The length for each session is 60 to 90 minutes.

Organizing

Facilitators: Have lay people facilitate the Bible studies, rather than clergy and other church staff members. If necessary, members of the council or governing board of the congregation can serve as facilitators, but it is better to utilize others in the congregation. Carefully recruit persons who can invite God's Spirit to guide the discussion—those who are mature in faith and interested in building up the body of Christ.

Hosts: Select and recruit hosts to welcome people with genuine hospitality and warmth. Ideally, these are different people than the facilitators. Food is not a necessary component, but may be provided.

Small groups: To set up the small groups, provide a variety of days, times, dates, facilitators, and locations. Invite people to select the session that works with their schedule. Another option is to assign everyone in the congregation to neighborhood groups and mail out a list of the groups. This might work better in smaller congregation or in congregations that have high involvement from their members. Allow for people to change groups if necessary.

Follow up: Make arrangements to follow up with those who don't sign up for a group or don't attend after they have signed up. The strategic planning team, facilitators, or hosts can make these contacts. A call from the host or facilitator before the first session is also helpful.

Training

Gather the facilitators for training, perhaps in a home. Hosts also can be invited to attend the training. If the group is larger than twelve, break into small groups. Distribute copies of the participants' sheets for the series and work through each session. Even though people might already know each other, it is helpful here and in the small groups to do the "getting acquainted"activities as warm-ups for more in-depth discussions. When it comes time for other activities (blessing cards, confession cards, the setting of goals, and so on), allow time for just a few ideas to surface. The goal is to expose the facilitators to the flow of the lesson plan, but not to complete all activities. Take a break after each of the Bible study sessions. After you have completed all three sessions, distribute the facilitator guide sheets (pages 89-94).

Chapter 3 Tool

Bible Study Series for Small Groups

Participant Sheets

Session 1:
What is the purpose of the church?

Opening prayer

Getting acquainted

Exploring Scripture

Read John 13. The setting for this passage is the last supper of Jesus with his disciples. At this meal, Jesus gave his followers some instructions (verses 14-15). What were they?

- What did Jesus mean by these words to the disciples?

- What do these words mean for us today?

Read John 13:34-35. These are words from a man who is aware that he is about to die. Final words often carry much weight.

- What is the new commandment given by Jesus?

- Why is it important to Jesus that "everyone will know that you are my disciples, if you have love for one another"?

Read Matthew 28:16-20. This section includes the "Great Commission." In these final words of Jesus to his disciples, what does Jesus ask his disciples to do?

Read Acts 1:6-8. The book of Acts is a continuation of the Gospel of Luke, written by the same author. Jesus gathers his followers together for final instruction. What does he ask them to do?

Pulling it together

- In the scripture passages for this session, what is the theme of the final words of Jesus?

- Why do you think Jesus cares so much about making disciples?

- Why does Jesus still care about making disciples today?

- How are the final words of Jesus still relevant for disciples today?

- Has the purpose of the church changed over time? Refer back to the Bible passages.

Making the connection

If your congregation has a mission statement, review it at this time. How is your congregation's mission statement consistent (or inconsistent) with Jesus' final instructions?

Celebrate ways the congregation lives out its mission. Celebrate ways your congregation has been a blessing to you and to others.

For the next session

Ponder the following question: Our congregation has been blessed, but how have we fallen short of reaching our mission? How could we expand our mission? (Be specific.)

Closing prayer

Session 2: Blessings and confessions

Opening prayer

Getting acquainted

Exploring Scripture

Read Acts 2:1-24. After Jesus ascended, his followers stayed in Jerusalem and devoted themselves to prayer (Acts 2:12-14). No doubt they were still sorting out the recent events involving Jesus: his crucifixion, resurrection, and ascension. The time was Pentecost, an annual festival for the spring harvest. Jews from many lands, speaking many languages, gathered in Jerusalem to offer their words of thanksgiving. The disciples were filled with God's Spirit and began to speak in languages they had never learned.

Peter's sermon stands in stark contrast with his earlier denial of Jesus. (See John 18:15-18, 25-27.) Peter denied Jesus on the night of his betrayal, yet Peter was blessed on Pentecost. Others were blessed through Peter's proclamation. Look at Acts 2:41-42 to learn how many people welcomed Peter's message, believed, and were baptized.

- Read Acts 10:1—11:18. What were the issues Peter struggled with?

- Review Acts 10:34; Acts 10:47; and Acts 11:17.

- What might it have meant for the early church to realize that God shows no partiality?

- In your opinion, was the early church restricting the message? If so, how?

- How was Peter hindering God (Acts 11:17)?

Pulling it together

- Can we relate to Peter?

- Do we in our own lives ever hinder or block God? If so, how?

Making the connection

How has our congregation hindered God's vision from becoming a reality?

For the next session

Keep in mind the final words of Jesus (studied in session 1) and the mission of the church. How are we to carry out God's mission for the church in our congregation? What is God calling us to do? (Be as specific as possible.)

Closing prayer

Session 3: Setting goals

Opening prayer

Getting acquainted

Exploring Scripture

Read Acts 28:16-31. Paul felt called by God's Spirit to take the gospel message to Rome. Acts 27 describes Paul setting sail for Rome. Violent storms forced Paul's boat to be shipwrecked. Three months later, Paul set sail again and finally arrived in Rome.

In this passage, we read about Paul's arrest in Jerusalem and the opposition he faced from the Jews. None of the local Jewish leaders in Rome had heard about Paul, so a meeting was arranged. Paul shared his faith and met a mixed reaction. Some believed and others did not. Nevertheless, Paul lived in Rome for two years (Acts 28:30), "proclaiming the kingdom of God and teaching about the Lord Jesus Christ with all boldness and without hindrance" (Acts 28:31). Why did Paul keep on proclaiming the faith despite persecution and hardship?

Pulling it together

- Have you every done something bold for the faith?

- How might we as individual people be bolder in our witness to Christ?

- How might we as a congregation be bolder in our witness to Christ?

Making the connection

What is God calling this congregation to do and to be?

Closing prayer

Bible Study Series for Small Groups

Facilitator Guide

Session 1:
What is the purpose of the church?

Objectives: To spend time in prayer and study to discern God's vision for the congregation, get acquainted with others in the small group, discern the purpose of the church by studying the final instructions of Jesus in the Bible, and celebrate blessings received through the ministry of the congregation.

Supplies: Bibles, pens or pencils, a "blessing card" for each person. For blessing cards, write the following words on brightly colored cardstock: "BLESSINGS—Ways you and others have been blessed through the ministry of our congregation."

Opening prayer

Getting acquainted

Invite each person to share the story of how he or she came to your congregation.

Exploring Scripture

Invite people to open their Bibles to John 13. Read this chapter like a play. Ask for volunteers to read parts: the narrator, Simon Peter, Jesus, and the disciple whom Jesus loved (verses 23-25).

At this meal, Jesus gave his followers some instructions. What were they? (To wash one another's feet, to be an example.)

Read John 13:34-35. Why is it important to Jesus that "everyone will know that you are my disciples, if you have love for one another"?

Read Matthew 28:16-20. This section includes the "Great Commission." In these final words of Jesus to his disciples, what does Jesus ask his disciples to do? (Go, make disciples, baptize, teach, and remember.)

Read Acts 1:6-8. The book of Acts is a continuation of the Gospel of Luke, written by the same author. Jesus gathers his followers together for final instruction. What does he ask them to do? (Be witnesses.)

Pulling it together

In the scripture passages for this session, what is the theme of the final words of Jesus? (Witness; love; make disciples.)

Has the purpose of the church changed over time? (The overall purpose of the church does not change over time, but the opportunities for the church to carry out its mission do change.)

Optional activity: What makes someone a disciple of Jesus? Create a "help wanted ad" for the ideal disciple. Describe what a church full of ideal disciples would be like.

Making the connection

If your congregation does not have a mission statement, begin to list phrases and words which seem vital for a mission statement of a congregation. Collect these and give them to members of the strategic planning team.

Distribute a "blessing card" to each person. Ask the group to silently list ways God has blessed them and others through the work of the congregation. Be sure to explain that these cards will be taken to the church and displayed. Collect the cards and return them to the church office.

For the next session

Closing prayer

End with the Lord's Prayer.

Follow up

Here are some ways for your congregation to use the blessing cards:

- Post on a kiosk in a narthex or gathering area.

- Display on a bulletin board for all to enjoy.

- Use as part of the prayers of thanks at a Sunday worship service.

- Compile a list of blessings to read at the next Bible study session.

- Create a mobile to display in the church building.

Session 2: Blessings and confessions

Objectives: To spend time in prayer and study to discern God's vision for the congregation, study a time of discernment for the early church, and confess falling short of God's mission for our congregation.

Supplies: Bibles, pens or pencils, a "confession card" for each person. For confession cards, write the following words on gray cardstock: "Confession—Ways our congregation has not been faithful to God's vision."

Opening prayer

Getting acquainted

Invite each person to share a brief description of the church where he or she was baptized.

Exploring Scripture

Invite people to open their Bibles to Acts 2:1-24.

Read Acts 10:1—11:18. Suggestion—Read this chapter like a play. Ask for volunteers to read parts: the narrator, Cornelius, angel of God/voice of God/Spirit, Peter, the men, and the circumcised believers (Acts 11:2). What were the issues Peter struggled with? (Eating unclean food, whether or not the gospel message and baptism were intended for Gentiles or just for the Jews.)

Pulling it together

Making the connection

Distribute the confession cards. Ask group members to silently and prayerfully list ways the congregation has hindered, blocked or fallen short of the mission of Jesus for the church. Be sure to explain that these cards will be taken to the church. Don't write any names on the cards. Collect the cards and return them to the church office.

Invite group members to share the confessions. What themes (or consistent phrases) are mentioned? How does it feel to know we have fallen short of God's mission? What is the role of forgiveness in all of this? (Allows us to confess, but also to trust that we are forgiven to move forward in Christ Jesus.) End on a positive note: People have been blessed through the ministry of the congregation, but there is much yet to be done.

For the next session

Closing prayer

End with the Lord's Prayer.

Follow up

Here are some ways for your congregation to use the confession cards:

- Lift them up to God as part of a worship service.

- Make a cross out of wood. Drive a long nail through the back at the center, so the nail sticks out at the front of the cross. Collect the confession cards and place them loosely on the nail. Burn the edges of the papers with a match or lit candle so that the pages curl up to create a rose shape. We offer our confessions to God and in Christ we are forgiven and set free. God can bring good and blessings out of our shortcomings. Warning: This can create a lot of smoke, particularly if the paper has film or wax on it. It may help to use nothing heavier than 20-pound paper for the confession cards.

Session 3: Setting goals

Objectives: To spend time in prayer and study to discern God's vision for the congregation, study an example of Paul's bold mission activities, and prayerfully consider goals for our congregation.

Supplies: Bibles, pens or pencils, large sheets of writing paper, and markers.

Opening prayer

Getting acquainted

Invite each person to share something daring and bold he or she has done in life.

Exploring Scripture

Invite people to open their Bibles to Acts 28:16-31.

Pulling it together

Making the connection

What is God calling this congregation to do and to be? List goals on large sheets of paper. Be specific. As a group, try to identify two goals that have the highest priority. Allow plenty of time for this activity. When done, celebrate the work of the group.

Closing prayer

End with the Lord's Prayer.

Follow up

- Arrange to display the goals generated by all the small groups.
- Compile the goals from all the groups and submit them to the strategic planning team to use in finalizing goals for the congregation.

Chapter 3 Tool

Fulfilling Our Purposes

Look at your congregation's mission and ministry in terms of the mission statement and purposes established by your denomination. The six purposes listed here are from the *Model Constitution for Congregations of the Evangelical Lutheran Church in America*, C4.02., but the same process could be adapted for use with other denominational constitutions.

1. Worship God in proclamation of the Word and administration of the sacraments and through lives of prayer, praise, thanksgiving, witness, and service.

   What the congregation is doing: _____

   _____

   How this mission and ministry could be expanded: _____

   _____

2. Proclaim God's saving gospel of justification by grace for Christ's sake through faith alone, according to the apostolic witness in the Holy Scripture, preserving and transmitting the gospel faithfully to future generations.

   What the congregation is doing: _____

   _____

   How this mission and ministry could be expanded: _____

   _____

3. Carry out Christ's Great Commission by reaching out to all people to bring them to faith in Christ and by doing all ministry with a global awareness consistent with the understanding of God as Creator, Redeemer, and Sanctifier of all.

What the congregation is doing: _____

_____

How this mission and ministry could be expanded: _____

_____

4. Serve in response to God's love to meet human needs, caring for the sick and the aged, advocating dignity and justice for all people, working for peace and reconciliation among the nations, and standing with the poor and powerless, and committing itself to their needs.

What the congregation is doing: _____

_____

How this mission and ministry could be expanded: _____

_____

5. Nurture its members in the Word of God so as to grow in faith and hope and love, to see daily life as the primary setting for the exercise of their Christian calling, and to use the gifts of the Spirit for their life together and for their calling in the world.

What the congregation is doing: _____

_____

How this mission and ministry could be expanded: _____

_____

6. Manifest the unity given to the people of God by living together in the love of Christ and by joining with other Christians in prayer and action to express and preserve the unity which the Spirit gives.

What the congregation is doing: _____

_____

How this mission and ministry could be expanded: _____

_____

Chapter 4 Tool

Mapping the Needs of Your Neighborhood

1. On a separate sheet of paper, place a symbol for your home at one edge of the page. Next, place a symbol for your church building at the opposite edge of the page.

2. Draw a map from your home to the church building, identifying the businesses, neighborhoods, schools, and hospitals along the way. (A rough sketch will be sufficient.)

3. List some of the needs evident in the places included on your map.

4. Share your list with a partner or small group. Add to your list if you wish.

5. Offer a brief prayer (silently or aloud) for those in need along the routes shown on your maps.

6. In a large group, combine the lists of needs you have identified. (You may want to verify these needs with information from the local school or school district office, Chamber of Commerce, social service agencies, or a neighborhood canvass.)

7. How will the congregation proclaim God's word and share God's love in this time and place? As witnesses for Christ, what goals could you set?

Chapter 5 Tool

Action Plan Worksheet

1. What is your congregation's mission statement? _____

_____

_____

_____

_____

_____

_____

_____

2. Write down one of your congregation's goals. _____

_____

_____

_____

3. What needs to happen? List the steps that need to be taken to reach this goal. _____

_____

_____

_____

_____

4. How will this be done? _____

_____

_____

_____

_____

5. Why will this be done? _____

_____

_____

_____

_____

6. Who will have primary responsibility for implementing the steps?

_____

_____

_____

7. Which resources will be used? Identify the financial resources, equipment, and so on that are needed. Are these resources available now or will they need to be obtained?

_____

_____

_____

_____

_____

8. When and where will the steps be completed? Identify the time-line for completion and (if needed) the location.

_____

_____

_____

_____

_____

_____

9. Evaluation: When will progress reports be given? How will you know that the goal has been reached?

_____

_____

_____

_____

_____

_____

Chapter 8 Tool

A Season of the Church Year

STOP

1. Call people to prayer.
2. Announce the planning process utilizing images of the church season.
3. Plan a significant worship celebration to launch the strategic planning process. (See "Worship Resources" and "A Liturgy of Blessing and Commissioning" on pages 71-79.)

LOOK

4. Arrange small group Bible studies (see pages 82-94) to focus on the mission mandate of Christ. These Bible studies were developed for small groups but can be adapted for use in a sermon series, large groups or personal devotions.
5. Include blessings and confessions as part of the process.

LISTEN

6. Pray for guidance concerning God's vision for your congregation.
7. Seek ways to LISTEN to the needs of the congregation and community.
8. Create preliminary goals as part of the small group discussions.
9. Gather the congregation for a large group session. Celebrate the work done in the small groups and reflect on the preliminary goals. Add any new goals to the list.
10. Prioritize goals.

GO

11. Form a task force to organize the work of the congregation into a systematic plan that reflects the mission mandate.

12. Get affirmation for the goals from the council or governing board and the congregation.

13. Allow the task force to create a feasible action plan to implement the goals. Indicate the person(s) or committee(s) who will have primary responsibility.

14. Celebrate the work of God within your congregation.

Chapter 8 Tool

A One-Day Planning Session

Preparation

- Invite an individual or group in the congregation to lead prayers throughout the day that ask for God's guidance. At each step along the way, turn to this individual or group to lead a time of prayer.

- Ask two people to serve as scribes, one to write down responses on a flip chart and the other to keep notes for the strategic planning team.

- Photocopy Session 1 in the small group Bible studies, pages 84-85 for each person.

Prelude:
Preparing to worship, plan, and pray

Leader: The Holy Spirit has gathered us together today to do the liturgy, the work of the people of God. Christ has called us to be his witnesses in the world. Today we will reflect upon that calling and plan how we can be faithful as followers of Christ. Let us pray for God's guidance and blessing as we begin.

Opening hymn

Call to worship (See "Worship Resources," pages 71-73)

Confession:
We STOP to acknowledge our failings

Gospel reading: Acts 1:1-4, 14

L: Before beginning the mission work to which they were called, Jesus told the disciples to STOP, wait, and Pray. We, too, prepare for our task by taking time for prayer and confession.

An exercise or prayer of confession

Words of absolution

Praise:
We STOP to give thanks for blessings

A hymn of praise

The kyrie

Speak the kyrie, and after each petition, ask what needs are being spoken "for the peace of the world, for this holy house," and so on. Write down the responses.

The collect: The prayer of the day

(Use the "Prayer for the planning process" on page 71, or use a similar prayer.)

Scripture: We LOOK to God's word

(In small groups, work through Session 1 from the "Bible Study Series for Small Groups," pages 84-85. Think about this question: "What do you hear God calling this congregation to be?" Then, in the large group, list your responses.)

Brief meditation or sermon

Break for lunch or refreshments

(The strategic planning team will look at the words and phrases that have been gathered and group similar items together in a new list to be displayed later.)

Prayers of the church:
We LISTEN to Jesus and to the community

(See "Prayers of the church" in "Worship Resources," page 72)

The offering: Our response to God's word

(Display the phrases listed from the kyrie and Bible study. Discuss in small groups: How can we respond to the needs? What gifts do we have to offer? Write down all responses. The strategic planning team will use these responses to begin formulating either a mission statement or goals.)

Holy Communion: We are nourished for service

Benediction and sending:
We GO to witness and serve

Chapter 8 Tool

A Prayer Retreat

Preparation: Cut out huge letters from poster board spelling "C-H-U-R-C-H."

Supplies: markers, scissors, glue, tape, and scraps of paper, fabric, and cardboard. For each participant, photocopy sessions 1-3 in the small group Bible studies on pages 84-88 and have three adhesive colored dots available.

Day 1

Supper or refreshments

STOP

Opening

- Begin with prayer, devotions, and singing.

- Distribute the C-H-U-R-C-H letters and markers. Invite people to remember their early experiences with "church" and draw something representing those experiences on the letters. When done, post the letters around the meeting area.

- Invite the participants to get into small groups with people they do not know well and create a "church" using scissors, glue, tape, and scraps. Provide time to view the results.

LOOK

Bible Study Session 1: "What Is The Purpose of the Church?"

Use the Getting Acquainted activities, then assemble in small groups for study and discussion. (It would be advisable to keep people in the same small groups for the entire retreat.)

Evening worship

Use the "Worship Resources" (pages 71-73).

Day 2

Breakfast and a brief devotional time

Bible Study Session 2: "Blessings and Confessions"

Study and discuss Session 2 in small groups and present the confessions to God in worship. Provide some time to wander, ponder, pray, and study.

Lunch

LISTEN

Bible Study Session 3: "Setting Goals"

Have small groups list their goals on large pieces of paper. Make these goals specific. Discuss goals in the large group. Then take a break, pray, and discern. What is God calling the congregation to do?

Prioritizing goals

Distribute adhesive dots. Ask that each person place dots on the top three goals he or she believes God is calling the congregation to establish. Note the priorities that emerge.

GO

Final worship

Conclude your time together with a worship celebration.

Follow-up after the retreat

- Fine-tune the language of the goals and publicize them.

- Give the congregation opportunities to review the goals and approve them.

- Expand the goals through the development of action plans.

Chapter 8 Tool

A Yearlong Process Involving Resource People

The summer could serve as a time of preparation, allowing the strategic planning process to become part of the congregation's fall activities. Begin by identifying and inviting persons to serve on the strategic planning team. These people can be identified by the congregation council, pastor, and lay leaders using the guidelines suggested in chapter 1.

Throughout the year of strategic planning, communicate what's happening with reports from the strategic planning team at each congregation council and committee meeting and in newsletters and bulletins. Include the strategic planning process in the prayers of the congregation.

STOP—Fall

- Introduce the approach and enlist support and commitment for the strategic planning process. (This commitment could be very specific, such as a commitment to participate in a Lenten Bible Study or to daily pray for the congregation's ministry.)

- Install or commission the strategic planning team during Sunday worship.

This time frame model on pages 110 to 112 is adapted from a two-year strategic planning process conducted at St. Paul Evangelical Lutheran Church, Baton Rouge, Louisiana, from 1993 to 1995.

- Have the strategic planning team review the present mission statement of the congregation, if there is one. Review the mission statement of your denomination and synod or judicatory.

- Identify the time frame and theme to be used in the strategic planning process.

- Set aside time for intentional prayer. See chapter 2 for ways to call the congregation to prayer.

- Set aside an all-committees night, a congregation council meeting, a youth meeting, and a Sunday school session to identify blessings and confessions. Have members of the strategic planning team serve as scribes at these meetings.

LOOK—Spring

- Reflect upon the mission and ministry of the congregation. The small group Bible studies (pages 82-94) could be used as the basis for mid-week Lenten services.

- Through prayer, Bible study, and conversations from meetings about blessings and confessions, begin to look and listen for key words, phrases, and themes. Have the strategic planning team gather these into a draft mission statement that articulates the mission mandate in the language of the congregation.

- Present this draft statement to committees and the congregation council. Publicize it in bulletins, newsletters, and so forth.

- Present the draft statement for discussion and adoption at a special congregational meeting in the spring.

LISTEN—Summer

- Set goals based on the adopted mission statement. One Sunday each month could be dedicated to a certain theme of the mission statement. Focus on the theme in worship and offer a time for fellowship and discussion (perhaps a potluck lunch). If desired, outside speakers and resource persons could be enlisted for these days.

- Listen to the needs and concerns of the congregation. Listen to the needs and concerns of the community.

GO—Fall

- Have all committees meet together to identify goals that reflect the mission statement. Have each committee rank their goals in order of significance.

- Communicate these goals to the congregation and provide times for discussion.

- Present these goals for discussion at the congregation's annual meeting. Identify goals for the coming year, for three years, and for five years. Commit to the goals as part of the meeting.

- Identify specific committees that will take responsibility for oversight of each goal.

- Include a review of the mission statement, an evaluation of the action plans, a celebration of goals reached, and a re-commitment to the mission and vision in each year's annual meeting.